Imagine a World..:
Self Paced Curriculum
by

Indana Simonde

ISBN: 9798852228192

Future of Humanity Act

Section 1: Purpose and Scope

1.1 Purpose:
This law aims to ensure the long-term well-being, sustainability, and ethical progress of humanity, both on Earth and in space. It establishes a framework for responsible governance, equitable resource management, environmental stewardship, technological advancement, and the promotion of human rights.

1.2 Scope:
This law applies to all individuals, organizations, and governing bodies that have a direct or indirect impact on the future of humanity. It encompasses activities on Earth, in space, and in any extraterrestrial environments that humans may explore or inhabit.

Section 2: Sustainable Development and Environmental Stewardship

2.1 Environmental Protection:
All activities shall be conducted in a manner that minimizes harm to the environment, mitigates climate change, and preserves biodiversity. Efforts shall be made to promote sustainable practices, reduce resource consumption, and prioritize renewable energy sources.

2.2 Conservation and Restoration:
Efforts shall be made to conserve and restore ecosystems, natural habitats, and biodiversity. Conservation initiatives should aim to protect endangered species, preserve ecological balance, and maintain the integrity of natural environments.

2.3 Responsible Resource Management:
The extraction, utilization, and distribution of natural resources shall be conducted in a manner that ensures their sustainable availability for future generations. Resource allocation should be equitable, considering the needs of both present and future populations.

Section 3: Technological Advancement and Ethical Innovation

3.1 Ethical Research and Development:
Technological advancements shall be pursued in a manner that prioritizes ethical considerations and respects human rights. Research and development activi-

ties should adhere to established ethical standards and consider potential social, economic, and environmental impacts.

3.2 Responsible AI and Robotics:
The development and deployment of artificial intelligence (AI) and robotics shall be governed by principles that prioritize safety, transparency, and accountability. Measures shall be taken to prevent AI misuse, ensure privacy, and avoid the creation of autonomous systems that pose risks to humanity.

3.3 Bioethics and Genetic Engineering:
Advancements in genetic engineering and biotechnology shall be conducted with consideration for ethical guidelines. The rights, dignity, and privacy of individuals shall be respected, and efforts shall be made to prevent unauthorized or unethical manipulation of human genetic material.

Section 4: Human Rights and Social Equality

4.1 Human Rights:
The protection and promotion of fundamental human rights, as outlined in international conventions and treaties, shall be a priority. Discrimination, exploitation, and any form of infringement upon human rights shall be strictly prohibited.

4.2 Social Equality:
Efforts shall be made to promote social equality, eliminate discrimination, and ensure equal access to opportunities, resources, and services. Measures shall be taken to reduce disparities in wealth, education, healthcare, and basic necessities among all individuals.

Section 5: International Collaboration and Peaceful Cooperation

5.1 International Cooperation:
Governments, organizations, and individuals shall actively engage in international collaboration, scientific exchange, and peaceful cooperation to address global challenges and promote the collective well-being of humanity.

5.2 Conflict Resolution:
Disputes and conflicts shall be resolved through diplomatic negotiations, dialogue, and nonviolent means. Efforts shall be made to promote disarmament, reduce the threat of nuclear weapons, and seek peaceful resolutions to conflicts that may arise.

Section 6: Governance and Implementation

6.1 Implementation and Enforcement:
National and international governing bodies shall enact legislation, regulations, and mechanisms to implement and enforce the provisions of this law. Adequate resources shall be allocated to ensure effective implementation, monitoring, and enforcement of the law's provisions.

6.2 Review and Amendments:
The law shall be subject to periodic review to assess its effectiveness and adapt to changing circumstances. Amendments may be made as necessary to ensure the law remains relevant and responsive to the evolving needs and challenges of humanity.

Conclusion:

The Future of Humanity Act establishes a comprehensive framework for responsible governance, sustainable development, ethical innovation, and the promotion of human rights. By adhering to the principles outlined in this law, humanity can strive towards a future that prioritizes the well-being, harmony, and long-term survival of all individuals and the ecosystems they inhabit.

Future of Humanity Academy

Mission:
The Future of Humanity Academy is dedicated to educating and inspiring individuals to understand and actively shape the future of humanity in alignment with the principles and objectives outlined in the Future of Humanity Act. The academy aims to cultivate a deep understanding of the ethical, scientific, and social dimensions of our collective future, fostering responsible leadership and promoting positive change.

Curriculum:

1. Core Principles of the Future of Humanity Act:
Students will study the foundational principles outlined in the Future of Humanity Act, exploring the importance of sustainability, environmental stewardship, technological advancement, human rights, social equality, and international cooperation. They will gain a comprehensive understanding of the Act's scope and how it applies to various aspects of human existence.

2. Sustainable Development and Environmental Sciences:

This curriculum focuses on the study of sustainable development practices, environmental sciences, and ecological conservation. Students will learn about the challenges facing our planet, the impact of human activities, and strategies for mitigating environmental degradation. They will explore solutions for achieving sustainable resource management and protecting biodiversity.

3. Ethical Technology and Innovation:
Students will delve into the ethical dimensions of technological advancements, including artificial intelligence, robotics, genetic engineering, and emerging technologies. They will examine the ethical implications of these technologies, discussing responsible development, privacy concerns, and the impact on human rights. They will explore case studies, engage in debates, and develop frameworks for ethical decision-making.

4. Human Rights and Social Justice:
This curriculum focuses on human rights, social equality, and inclusivity. Students will study international human rights laws, the history of social justice movements, and contemporary challenges related to discrimination, inequality, and systemic biases. They will develop an understanding of the importance of human rights and work towards promoting social equality and justice in their communities.

5. International Relations and Peace Studies:
Students will explore the field of international relations, studying diplomatic negotiations, conflict resolution, and the promotion of peaceful cooperation. They will examine global challenges, such as nuclear disarmament, climate change, and resource allocation, and learn strategies for effective diplomacy, fostering collaboration, and addressing conflicts through nonviolent means.

6. Future Studies and Futurism:
This curriculum will introduce students to the field of future studies and futurism, exploring scenarios for the future of humanity. Students will examine technological trends, demographic changes, and emerging possibilities, developing critical thinking skills to anticipate and shape the future. They will engage in scenario planning, forecasting techniques, and ethical considerations for future developments.

7. Capstone Project:
Students will undertake a capstone project that integrates the knowledge and skills gained throughout their studies. They will identify a specific issue or challenge related to the future of humanity and propose actionable solutions or

initiatives aligned with the principles of the Future of Humanity Act. They present their projects to peers, faculty, and external stakeholders.

Graduates of the Future of Humanity Academy will be equipped with the knowledge, skills, and ethical perspectives necessary to become leaders and change agents in shaping a sustainable, equitable, and ethically responsible future for humanity. By fostering interdisciplinary learning, critical thinking, and a global perspective, the academy aims to inspire a new generation of leaders committed to the well-being and long-term survival of our planet and its inhabitants.

Curriculum: Future Studies and Responsible Governance

Semester 1: Foundations of the Future

1. Introduction to Future Studies:
   - Understanding the field of future studies
   - Key concepts, methodologies, and frameworks
   - Examining different perspectives on the future

2. Sustainable Development and Environmental Stewardship:
   - Principles of sustainable development
   - Environmental sciences and conservation
   - Strategies for sustainable resource management

3. Ethics of Technological Advancement:
   - Ethical considerations in emerging technologies
   - Responsible AI and robotics
   - Bioethics and genetic engineering

4. Human Rights and Social Justice:
   - International human rights laws and treaties
   - Equality, diversity, and inclusivity
   - Addressing systemic biases and promoting social justice

Semester 2: Shaping the Future

1. International Relations and Peaceful Cooperation:
   - Diplomatic negotiations and conflict resolution
   - Global challenges and collaborative solutions
   - Building peaceful and cooperative relationships

2. Responsible Governance and Policy Development:
   - Principles of responsible governance
   - Policy-making for sustainable development
   - Promoting transparency, accountability, and citizen participation

3. Future Technologies and Innovation:
   - Futuristic technologies and their potential impacts
   - Ethical frameworks for technological innovation
   - Anticipating and managing technological disruptions

4. Interstellar Exploration and Ethical Considerations:
   - Challenges and possibilities of interstellar travel
   - Ethical considerations for space exploration
   - Governance and regulations for future space activities

Semester 3: Creating the Future

1. Scenario Planning and Futures Thinking:
   - Scenario development and analysis
   - Critical thinking for future planning
   - Evaluating uncertainties and possibilities

2. Capstone Project - Future Scenarios:
   - Collaborative group project
   - Developing and presenting future scenarios
   - Addressing ethical, social, and environmental implications

3. Leadership and Responsible Decision-Making:
   - Ethical leadership principles
   - Responsible decision-making in complex environments
   - Balancing stakeholder interests and long-term goals

4. Communication and Advocacy for the Future:
   - Effective communication strategies for future issues
   - Advocacy for sustainable development and responsible governance
   - Engaging stakeholders and fostering public support

Note: This curriculum provides a comprehensive framework for future studies and responsible governance, integrating elements of sustainability, ethics, human rights, technological advancement, and global cooperation. Each semester builds on the previous one, culminating in a capstone project that applies the knowledge and skills acquired throughout the program. The curriculum encourages critical thinking, interdisciplinary learning, and proactive engagement with the challenges and opportunities of the future.

Free Astrology Course (1 Semester)

Week 1: Introduction to Astrology
- Overview of astrology as a study of cosmic influences
- Historical development and cultural variations of astrology
- Basic concepts: zodiac signs, planets, houses, and aspects

Week 2: Birth Charts and Natal Astrology
- Understanding birth charts and their components
- Interpretation of zodiac signs, planets, and houses in a natal chart
- Identifying personality traits and potential life patterns through astrology

Week 3: Planetary Influences
- Exploration of the planets and their symbolic meanings
- Understanding planetary aspects and their effects on personality and life events
- Case studies and practical applications of planetary influences

Week 4: Zodiac Signs and Personality Traits
- In-depth study of the twelve zodiac signs and their characteristics
- Interpreting zodiac sign placements in a birth chart
- Exploring the influences of zodiac signs on personality traits and behavior

Week 5: Houses and Life Areas
- Understanding the twelve houses in astrology and their significance
- Interpreting house placements in a birth chart
- Examining the different life areas represented by each house

Week 6: Predictive Astrology: Transits and Progressions
- Introduction to predictive astrology methods
- Exploring transits and progressions and their influence on personal development
- Using transits and progressions to predict significant life events

Week 7: Synastry and Relationship Astrology
- Study of synastry, the comparison of birth charts for relationship analysis
- Understanding the dynamics between individuals based on astrology
- Interpretation of aspects and placements in relationship astrology

Week 8: Astrology and Career Guidance
- Applying astrology to career choices and vocational guidance
- Identifying talents, potentials, and suitable career paths through birth charts
- Case studies and practical exercises for career astrology

Week 9: Astrology and Health
- Examining the connections between astrology and health
- Identifying potential health challenges through birth charts
- Exploring alternative healing approaches based on astrological influences

Week 10: Ethical Considerations in Astrology
- Understanding the ethical responsibilities of astrologers
- Establishing boundaries and limitations in astrological practice
- Addressing potential pitfalls and misconceptions in astrology

Week 11-14: Practical Application and Case Studies
- Practicing chart interpretation and analysis
- Conducting mock consultations and providing feedback
- Engaging in group discussions and sharing experiences

Psychology Course (1 Semester)

Week 1: Introduction to Psychology
- Overview of the field of psychology and its major subfields
- Historical perspectives and milestones in psychology
- Scientific methods and ethical considerations in psychological research

Week 2: Biological Foundations of Behavior
- Understanding the structure and function of the nervous system
- Exploring the role of genetics and heredity in behavior
- Examining the influence of hormones and neurotransmitters on behavior and mental processes

Week 3: Cognitive Psychology
- Introduction to cognitive processes such as perception, attention, memory, and thinking
- Exploring cognitive development and information processing
- Cognitive biases and decision-making processes

Week 4: Developmental Psychology
- Examining human development across the lifespan
- Theories of development: Piaget, Erikson, and Kohlberg

- Socioemotional development, identity formation, and moral reasoning

Week 5: Social Psychology
- Understanding the influence of social interactions on behavior and attitudes
- Conformity, obedience, and group dynamics
- Stereotypes, prejudice, and interpersonal relationships

Week 6: Personality Theories
- Major theories of personality: Freud, Jung, and the Big Five model
- Personality assessment and measurement
- Exploring the stability and change of personality over time

Week 7: Abnormal Psychology
- Classification and diagnosis of psychological disorders
- Major categories of disorders and their symptoms
- Treatment approaches: psychotherapy, medications, and alternative therapies

Week 8: Motivation and Emotion
- Understanding human motivation: biological, psychological, and social factors
- Exploring the nature of emotions and their impact on behavior
- Theories of motivation and emotion: Maslow, Drive Theory, and Cannon-Bard Theory

Week 9: Learning and Behaviorism
- Principles of learning and behaviorism
- Classical conditioning, operant conditioning, and observational learning
- Behavior modification and applications of learning principles

Week 10: Sensation and Perception
- The process of sensation and perception
- Vision, hearing, taste, smell, and touch
- Perception of depth, illusions, and the role of attention

Week 11-14: Applied Psychology and Contemporary Issues
- Applications of psychology in various settings: clinical, organizational, educational, and forensic
- Current topics in psychology: positive psychology, multicultural psychology, and environmental psychology
- Exploring career paths and opportunities in psychology

Note: The suggested curricula provide an overview of the topics that could be covered in a semester-long free astrology course and a psychology course. However, the depth and specific content covered may vary depending on the level and scope of the courses.

Semester 1: Astronomy

Week 1: Introduction to Astronomy
- Overview of the field of astronomy
- Historical milestones and developments in astronomy
- Celestial coordinate systems and observational tools

Week 2: Foundations of Astronomy
- Celestial mechanics and Kepler's laws
- Gravity and the motion of celestial bodies
- The electromagnetic spectrum and telescopes

Week 3: The Solar System
- Overview of the Sun and its properties
- The planets, moons, asteroids, and comets in our solar system
- Comparative planetary geology and atmospheres

Week 4: Stars and Stellar Evolution
- Stellar properties and classifications
- Stellar formation, main sequence, and stellar evolution
- Stellar death: supernovae, white dwarfs, neutron stars, and black holes

Week 5: Galaxies and the Universe
- Types of galaxies: spiral, elliptical, and irregular
- Galactic structure and the Milky Way
- The expanding universe, redshift, and cosmic microwave background radiation

Week 6: Cosmology and the Big Bang Theory
- Introduction to cosmology and the study of the universe
- The Big Bang Theory and the early universe
- Dark matter, dark energy, and the fate of the universe

Week 7: Exoplanets and Astrobiology
- Detection methods and properties of exoplanets
- Habitability and the search for life beyond Earth
- Astrobiology: the origin of life and the conditions for habitability

Week 8: Stellar Astronomy and Observational Techniques
- Stellar spectra and classification
- Stellar evolution and the Hertzsprung-Russell diagram
- Observational techniques: photometry, spectroscopy, and astrometry

Week 9: Galactic Astronomy and Dark Matter
- Galactic structure and dynamics
- The concept of dark matter and its impact on galactic evolution
- Observational evidence for dark matter

Week 10: High-Energy Astronomy and Cosmology
- Introduction to high-energy astronomy: X-rays, gamma rays, and cosmic rays
- Active galactic nuclei, quasars, and black hole physics
- Cosmic microwave background radiation and its implications for cosmology

Week 11-14: Special Topics and Research
- Exploration of specific astronomical topics such as pulsars, supernovae, galaxy clusters, or gravitational waves
- Research projects or presentations on recent astronomical discoveries
- Engaging in observational activities, data analysis, or simulation exercises

Semester 2: Earth Geosciences

Week 1: Introduction to Earth Sciences
- Overview of Earth's structure and composition
- Earth's geological time scale and historical developments in geosciences
- The interdisciplinary nature of Earth sciences

Week 2: Plate Tectonics and Earth's Interior
- Plate tectonic theory and evidence
- Earth's internal structure and geophysical techniques
- Plate boundaries, earthquakes, and volcanism

Week 3: Minerals and Rocks
- Classification and properties of minerals
- Igneous, sedimentary, and metamorphic rocks
- Rock-forming processes and the rock cycle

Week 4: Earth's Surface Processes
- Weathering, erosion, and sedimentation
- River systems, glaciers, and coastal processes

- Mass movements and the shaping of landscapes

Week 5: Earth's Atmosphere and Climate
- Structure and composition of the atmosphere
- Climate systems and factors influencing climate change
- Weather patterns, atmospheric circulation, and climate modeling

Week 6: Earth's Oceans and Hydrosphere
- Oceanic structure and properties
- Ocean circulation, waves, and tides
- Coastal processes and marine ecosystems

Week 7: Earth's Paleoclimate and Climate Change
- The study of past climates through proxies
- Paleoclimate records and their implications for understanding climate change
- Human impacts on climate and mitigation strategies

Week 8: Earth's Resources: Minerals and Energy
- Earth's mineral resources and their extraction
- Fossil fuels, renewable energy sources, and their environmental impacts
- Sustainable resource management and conservation

Week 9: Geologic Time and Evolution of Life
- Geological time scale and the history of life on Earth
- Fossils and their significance in understanding evolution
- Mass extinctions and the role of geological events

Week 10: Environmental Geology and Natural Hazards
- Earthquakes, volcanic eruptions, and their hazards
- Landslides, floods, and other natural disasters
- Environmental geology and mitigating human impacts on the environment

Week 11-14: Fieldwork and Research
- Field trips to study geological formations, landforms, or environmental processes
- Research projects or presentations on specific geological topics
- Analyzing geological data, conducting experiments, or utilizing geospatial technologies

Note: This curriculum provides a comprehensive overview of topics that could be covered in a two-semester astronomy and earth geosciences course. The specific depth and content covered may vary based on the level and scope of the course. Practical components such as observational activities, laboratory work, and field trips are included to enhance hands-on learning and practical application of knowledge.

Semester 1: Fundamentals of Mathematics

Week 1: Introduction to Mathematics
- Overview of the importance and applications of mathematics
- Basic mathematical notation and terminology
- The role of logic and proof in mathematics

Week 2: Number Systems and Operations
- Introduction to different number systems: natural numbers, integers, rational numbers, and real numbers
- Operations: addition, subtraction, multiplication, and division
- Properties of numbers and their application in problem-solving

Week 3: Algebraic Expressions and Equations
- Simplifying algebraic expressions
- Solving linear equations and inequalities
- Formulating and solving word problems using algebraic equations

Week 4: Functions and Graphs
- Understanding functions and their representations
- Graphing linear and quadratic functions
- Exploring transformations of functions

Week 5: Exponents and Logarithms
- Laws of exponents and their applications
- Introduction to logarithmic functions and properties
- Solving exponential and logarithmic equations

Week 6: Geometry and Trigonometry
- Basic geometric concepts: points, lines, angles, and polygons
- Pythagorean theorem and its applications
- Introduction to trigonometric ratios and their applications

Week 7: Probability and Statistics
- Understanding probability and its applications
- Collecting and organizing data
- Descriptive statistics: measures of central tendency and dispersion

Week 8: Sequences and Series
- Arithmetic sequences and series
- Geometric sequences and series
- Applications of sequences and series in various contexts

Week 9: Matrices and Determinants
- Introduction to matrices and their operations
- Solving systems of linear equations using matrices
- Determinants and their properties

Week 10: Introduction to Calculus
- Limits and continuity
- Differentiation and its applications
- Introduction to integration

Week 11-14: Applications of Mathematics
- Applying mathematical concepts to real-world problems
- Exploring mathematical modeling
- Project-based learning and problem-solving exercises

Semester 2: Fibonacci Sequence and its Applications

Week 1: Introduction to Fibonacci Sequence
- Origin and history of the Fibonacci sequence
- Recursive definition and properties of the sequence
- Notable examples and patterns in the sequence

Week 2: Golden Ratio and Fibonacci Numbers
- Understanding the concept of the golden ratio
- Relationship between the golden ratio and Fibonacci numbers
- Applications of the golden ratio in art, architecture, and nature

Week 3: Fibonacci Sequence and Nature
- Exploring the presence of Fibonacci numbers in natural phenomena
- Fibonacci spiral and its occurrences in nature
- Examples of the Fibonacci sequence in plant growth patterns and animal structures

Week 4: Fibonacci Sequence in Mathematics
- Mathematical properties and proofs related to the Fibonacci sequence
- Fibonacci numbers and the Pascal's triangle
- Applications of Fibonacci numbers in number theory and combinatorics

Week 5: Fibonacci Sequence in Geometry
- Fibonacci numbers and the Fibonacci spiral in geometric constructions
- Fibonacci rectangles and their properties
- Exploration of the relationship between the Fibonacci sequence and the golden rectangle

Week 6: Fibonacci Sequence in Music and Art
- Fibonacci numbers in musical composition and rhythm
- Fibonacci patterns in visual art and design
- Creative applications of the Fibonacci sequence in various art forms

Week 7: Fibonacci Sequence in Financial Markets
- Fibonacci retracements and extensions in technical analysis
- Fibonacci numbers and their significance in financial forecasting
- Application of Fibonacci sequence in investment strategies

Week 8: Fibonacci Sequence and Recurrence Relations
- Analyzing and solving recurrence relations using Fibonacci numbers
- Deriving explicit formulas for Fibonacci sequence terms
- Applications of recurrence relations in various mathematical contexts

Week 9: Fibonacci Sequence and Algorithms
- Fibonacci numbers in algorithm design and optimization
- Exploring algorithms that utilize the Fibonacci sequence
- Analyzing time complexity and efficiency of Fibonacci-based algorithms

Week 10: Fibonacci Sequence and Fractals
- Fibonacci numbers and their relation to fractals
- Construction of Fibonacci fractals and their properties
- Examining the self-similarity and intricate patterns in Fibonacci-based fractals

Week 11-14: Project-Based Learning and Exploration
- Undertaking individual or group projects related to the Fibonacci sequence
- Investigating specific applications or extensions of the sequence
- Presenting findings and engaging in discussions on the significance of the Fibonacci sequence

Note: This curriculum provides a comprehensive overview of the fundamentals of mathematics and the importance of the Fibonacci sequence. The specific depth and content covered may vary based on the level and scope of the course.

Practical components, such as problem-solving exercises, project-based learning, and real-world applications, are included to enhance understanding and foster a deeper appreciation for mathematics and the Fibonacci sequence.

**Towards Global Disarmament: Building a Peaceful Future**

Introduction:
In a world marked by conflicts and the proliferation of weapons, the need for global disarmament has become increasingly urgent. "Towards Global Disarmament: Building a Peaceful Future" explores the multifaceted reasons and principles behind the pursuit of disarmament. This book delves into the interplay of political ideologies, movements, and moral imperatives that underpin the quest for a world free from the scourge of violence and armed conflicts.

Chapter 1: The Imperative for Disarmament
- Examining the consequences of armed conflicts on societies, economies, and human lives.
- Analyzing the risks posed by the existence and use of weapons of mass destruction.
- The ethical imperative of promoting peace and non-violence.

Chapter 2: Philosophical Perspectives
- Exploring pacifism as a philosophical basis for global disarmament.
- Investigating the principles of non-violence and their application in international relations.
- Examining the intersection of disarmament and human rights.

Chapter 3: Global Governance and Multilateralism
- The role of international organizations in facilitating disarmament efforts.
- Analyzing the importance of multilateral diplomacy and cooperation.
- The United Nations and its disarmament initiatives.

Chapter 4: The Anti-Nuclear Movement
- Tracing the history and impact of the movement against nuclear weapons.
- Examining the dangers posed by nuclear arsenals and the call for their abolition.
- Evaluating disarmament treaties and the challenges they face.

Chapter 5: Humanitarianism and Disarmament
- Linking disarmament with humanitarian principles and the protection of human rights.
- Analyzing the devastating humanitarian consequences of armed conflicts.

- The role of disarmament in preventing civilian casualties and promoting humanitarian aid.

Chapter 6: Environmentalism and Disarmament
- Investigating the environmental impact of weapons production and warfare.
- Exploring the synergies between disarmament and sustainable development.
- The potential for environmental cooperation as a driver for disarmament.

Chapter 7: Paths to Disarmament
- Strategies for achieving global disarmament.
- Arms control agreements, confidence-building measures, and diplomatic initiatives.
- Disarmament in conflict-affected regions and post-conflict reconstruction.

Chapter 8: Overcoming Challenges
- Addressing the obstacles and resistance to disarmament efforts.
- Economic and political considerations in disarmament processes.
- The role of civil society, grassroots movements, and public awareness.

Conclusion:
In "Towards Global Disarmament: Building a Peaceful Future," we have explored the multitude of reasons, political ideologies, and movements that advocate for disarmament. By examining the imperative for peace, philosophical perspectives, global governance, the anti-nuclear movement, humanitarianism, environmentalism, and practical paths to disarmament, we lay the groundwork for envisioning a world where violence and armed conflicts are replaced with dialogue, cooperation, and sustainable development. Only through collective action can we transcend the challenges and build a peaceful future for all.

Forward:

In the realm of philosophical inquiry, the exploration of eternity and its intricate relationship with quantum temporal dynamics has captured the imagination of thinkers across time. In this groundbreaking essay, we embark on a thought-provoking journey that delves into the very nature of existence, time, and the eternal.

Drawing upon the principles of quantum mechanics and the intricate interplay between time and consciousness, this essay challenges conventional notions of temporality and expands our understanding of the eternal beyond linear constraints. By venturing into the depths of metaphysics and exploring the enigmatic nature of existence, we find ourselves on the precipice of a profound paradigm shift.

This essay contemplates the timeless nature of reality, probing the depths of quantum temporal dynamics and its implications for our perception of time. We question the boundaries of past, present, and future, and contemplate the potential interconnectedness of all moments within the eternal fabric of existence.

As we navigate the complexities of quantum mechanics, we are confronted with philosophical inquiries that transcend our conventional understanding of time. Through the lens of quantum temporal dynamics, we ponder the notion of a cyclical eternity, where time becomes an intricate tapestry of interconnected moments, perpetually unfolding in a cosmic dance.

This essay(s) challenge us to reconsider our preconceived notions of the universe as a linear progression and invites us to contemplate the infinite possibilities that arise from a deeper understanding of quantum temporal dynamics. It invites us to question the boundaries of causality and the potential for transformative shifts in our perception of reality.

By engaging with the profound concepts explored in this essay, we embark on a philosophical odyssey that illuminates the interconnectedness of all things. It is an invitation to expand our horizons, pushing the boundaries of human comprehension and embracing the awe-inspiring mysteries that lie beyond the veil of our limited perception.

As we journey through the intricacies of quantum temporal dynamics and its profound implications for the eternal, we are reminded of the boundless potential that lies within our collective consciousness. This essay serves as a catalyst for intellectual exploration, encouraging us to ponder the profound questions that have captivated philosophers throughout the ages.

In embracing this essay, we embark on an intellectual and philosophical adventure that challenges our assumptions, expands our horizons, and invites us to glimpse the eternal fabric that weaves through the tapestry of existence. It is an invitation to join the ongoing quest for knowledge, understanding, and the infinite wonders that lie beyond.

May this exploration into the depths of quantum temporal dynamics philosophy and its implications for eternity ignite the flames of curiosity, inspire contemplation, and open new vistas of insight as we journey together into the timeless realms that shape our understanding of existence.

The Earth's lifespan and the presence of humanity on it depend on a multitude of factors, including geological, ecological, and societal changes. The Earth itself has been around for approximately 4.5 billion years, and it is expected to remain habitable for several more billion years. However, the future of humanity on Earth depends on our ability to address various challenges, such as climate change, resource depletion, and sustainable practices. The exact duration that humanity will last on Earth is uncertain and depends on how we navigate these challenges. It requires taking proactive measures to mitigate the impact of human activities on the environment, develop sustainable technologies, and foster responsible stewardship of the planet. Scientists, policymakers, and individuals worldwide are actively working to address these issues and find ways to ensure the long-term sustainability of our planet. Through collective efforts, it is possible to extend the duration of human presence on Earth while preserving the Earth's ecosystems and ensuring a habitable environment for future generations. It is important to note that the future is shaped by numerous factors that are constantly evolving, and accurate long-term predictions are challenging. The actions we take today can significantly influence the duration of our presence on Earth, and it is up to us to make responsible choices and work towards a sustainable future.

**Disarmament**

1. Reduction of armed conflicts and their devastating consequences.
2. Preservation of human life and prevention of casualties.
3. Mitigation of the risk of nuclear war and the use of weapons of mass destruction.
4. Promotion of global peace and stability.
5. Fostering of trust and cooperation among all nations.
6. Allocation of resources toward social and economic development.
7. Advancement of education, healthcare, and poverty alleviation.
8. Protection of the environment from the negative impacts of weapons production and testing.
9. Reduction of military expenditures and the financial burden on nations.
10. Elimination of the threat posed by nuclear weapons.
11. Prevention of the proliferation of weapons of mass destruction.
12. Strengthening of international law and disarmament treaties.
13. Facilitation of conflict resolution through peaceful means.
14. Cultivation of a culture of non-violence and cooperation.
15. Promotion of human rights, dignity, and equality.
16. Empowerment of civil society and grassroots movements.
17. Protection of civilian populations from the devastating impacts of warfare.
18. Prevention of the suffering caused by armed conflicts.
19. Reconciliation and healing in post-conflict societies.
20. Advancement of dialogue and understanding between nations.
21. Preservation of cultural heritage and diversity.
22. Advancement of scientific research and innovation for peaceful purposes.

23. Exploration of space and the universe without militarization.
24. Promotion of disarmament education and awareness.
25. Reduction of the illegal arms trade and black market.
26. Decrease in the availability of weapons to non-state actors.
27. Reduction of violence and crime rates.
28. Prevention of terrorism and extremist ideologies.
29. Strengthening of international norms against the use of force.
30. Protection of children from the impact of armed conflict.
31. Prevention of forced displacement of populations due to warfare.
32. Promotion of sustainable development and resilience.
33. Respect for the principles of self-determination and sovereignty.
34. Preservation of infrastructure and cities from destruction.
35. Advancement of responsible and ethical behavior in international relations.
36. Cultivation of a sense of global citizenship and shared responsibility.
37. Facilitation of disarmament verification and inspections.
38. Reduction of the threat of cyber warfare.
39. Prevention of the militarization of police forces.
40. Promotion of non-military solutions to global challenges.
41. Protection of future generations from the legacy of warfare.
42. Promotion of disarmament in conflict-affected regions.
43. Prevention of the use of child soldiers.
44. Preservation of natural resources and ecosystems.
45. Promotion of economic stability and growth.
46. Reduction of regional tensions and conflicts.
47. Prevention of arms races and the escalation of tensions.
48. Advancement of gender equality and women's empowerment.
49. Strengthening of global governance and cooperation.
50. Promotion of diplomacy and peaceful resolution of disputes.

Please note that this list contains only a fraction of the potential reasons for global disarmament. The discourse on this topic encompasses numerous other perspectives and arguments.

While there isn't a specific school of political thought directly based on the above list of reasons for global disarmament, the principles and ideas expressed align with various existing ideologies and movements. Some of these include:

1. Pacifism: Pacifism is a philosophy that advocates for non-violence and opposes war and armed conflicts. It promotes the use of peaceful means to resolve disputes and emphasizes the preservation of human life and well-being.

2. Global Governance: The concept of global governance emphasizes the need for international cooperation and institutions to address global challenges and promote peace. It emphasizes the importance of multilateralism, diplomacy, and the rule of law in resolving conflicts and promoting disarmament.

3. Anti-Nuclear Movement: The anti-nuclear movement focuses specifically on the abolition of nuclear weapons and the prevention of nuclear war. It advocates for disarmament, arms control agreements, and the elimination of nuclear arsenals worldwide.

4. Humanitarianism: Humanitarianism places a strong emphasis on the protection of human rights, the prevention of suffering, and the promotion of human dignity. Disarmament aligns with the humanitarian principles of reducing violence and conflict to safeguard the well-being of individuals and communities.

5. Environmentalism: Environmentalism advocates for the protection of the environment and sustainable practices. Disarmament aligns with environmentalism by addressing the detrimental environmental impacts associated with weapons production, testing, and war.

It's important to note that these are broad categories, and there are various interpretations and subgroups within each. Additionally, the reasons for disarmament can be supported by a combination of different political ideologies and movements.

or

1. Reduction of violence and conflict.
2. Preservation of human life.
3. Prevention of war and its devastating consequences.
4. Mitigation of the risk of accidental or unauthorized use of weapons.
5. Promotion of global peace and stability.
6. Fostering of trust and cooperation among nations.
7. Allocation of resources toward social and economic development.
8. Advancement of education and healthcare.
9. Alleviation of poverty and inequality.
10. Protection of the environment from the impacts of weapons production and testing.
11. Reduction of military expenditures and the burden on national budgets.
12. Prevention of arms races and the escalation of tensions.
13. Elimination of the threat of nuclear weapons.
14. Prevention of the proliferation of weapons of mass destruction.

15. Creation of a safer and more secure world.
16. Enhancement of global governance and diplomacy.
17. Strengthening of international law and disarmament treaties.
18. Promotion of human rights and the rule of law.
19. Facilitation of conflict resolution through peaceful means.
20. Cultivation of a culture of non-violence and cooperation.
21. Empowerment of civil society and grassroots movements.
22. Protection of civilian populations from the impacts of warfare.
23. Prevention of the suffering caused by armed conflicts.
24. Reconciliation and healing in post-conflict societies.
25. Encouragement of dialogue and understanding between nations.
26. Preservation of cultural heritage and diversity.
27. Advancement of scientific research and innovation.
28. Exploration of space and the universe for peaceful purposes.
29. Prevention of the militarization of space.
30. Promotion of disarmament education and awareness.
31. Empowerment of women and promotion of gender equality.
32. Reduction of the illegal arms trade and black market.
33. Decrease in the availability of weapons to non-state actors.
34. Strengthening of international norms against the use of force.
35. Protection of children from the impact of armed conflict.
36. Prevention of the displacement of populations due to warfare.
37. Promotion of sustainable development and resilience.
38. Respect for the principles of self-determination and sovereignty.
39. Prevention of the destruction of infrastructure and cities.
40. Promotion of ethical behavior and responsibility in international relations.
41. Cultivation of a sense of global citizenship.
42. Facilitation of disarmament verification and inspections.
43. Reduction of the threat of terrorism and extremist ideologies.
44. Prevention of the militarization of police forces.
45. Advancement of non-military solutions to global challenges.
46. Protection of future generations from the legacy of warfare.
47. Promotion of disarmament in conflict-affected regions.
48. Prevention of the use of child soldiers.
49. Preservation of natural resources and ecosystems.
50. Prevention of the use of chemical and biological weapons.

## Means to Disarmament

1. Promotion of Peace: Disarmament can contribute to the reduction of conflicts and the promotion of peaceful relations among nations and civilisations within the solar system.

2. Mitigation of Risks: Removing weapons from the solar system can help mitigate the risk of accidental or unauthorised use, preventing catastrophic consequences.
3. Resource Reallocation: The resources spent on developing and maintaining weapons could be redirected toward addressing societal needs such as education, healthcare, poverty alleviation, and scientific research.
4. Preservation of Life: Disarmament can save countless lives by preventing armed conflicts and the destructive power of weapons.
5. Economic Advancement: Funds and resources devoted to arms races and military expenditures could be channeled into economic development, fostering prosperity and improving living conditions.
6. Environmental Protection: The production, testing, and deployment of weapons often have significant negative impacts on the environment. Disarmament can help preserve the delicate balance of ecosystems within the solar system.
7. Confidence Building: Disarmament can foster trust and cooperation between nations and civilizations, promoting dialogue and diplomacy as the primary means of resolving disputes.
8. Cultural Exchange: By focusing on disarmament, societies can foster cultural exchange and collaboration, promoting understanding, tolerance, and mutual respect.
9. Scientific Progress: Cooperation and resource sharing can enable greater scientific advancements and exploration of the solar system, expanding our knowledge of the universe.
10. Ethical Imperative: The pursuit of disarmament is aligned with the ethical principles of non-violence, respect for human dignity, and the preservation of life.

Please note that this list contains only a fraction of the potential reasons for disarmament. There are numerous other perspectives and arguments that contribute to the broader discourse on this topic.

The effect of an astronomical body, such as a large asteroid or comet, colliding with Earth would have significant consequences for existence and life on our planet. The severity of the impact depends on several factors, including the size, speed, and composition of the celestial object, as well as the location of the impact.

1. Immediate Impact:
The immediate effects of a large impact would be catastrophic. The force generated by the collision would result in an enormous release of energy, causing widespread destruction in the impact zone. The initial impact would cause

shockwaves, massive explosions, and the ejection of debris into the atmosphere.

2. Atmospheric Effects:
The impact would send vast amounts of dust, rock, and other materials into the atmosphere. This would create a dense cloud of debris that could block sunlight, leading to a significant decrease in global temperatures. The resulting reduction in sunlight would impact photosynthesis, potentially causing a decline in plant growth and disrupting food chains.

3. Global Climate Change:
The injection of large quantities of dust and gases into the atmosphere would have long-term effects on the global climate. The dust particles would scatter sunlight, further reducing temperatures and causing a prolonged period of darkness. The release of gases, such as sulfur compounds, could contribute to the formation of acid rain and further alter the climate patterns.

4. Extinction-Level Events:
Depending on the size and energy of the impact, there is a potential for mass extinctions. The collision of a large astronomical body with Earth could lead to widespread destruction of habitats, ecosystems, and species. Past events, such as the asteroid impact that caused the extinction of the dinosaurs, provide evidence of the devastating consequences of such collisions.

5. Geological Effects:
An impact of significant magnitude would generate powerful shockwaves that could trigger earthquakes, tsunamis, and volcanic activity. The impact's energy would be transferred into the Earth's crust, causing widespread seismic disturbances and altering geological structures.

6. Long-Term Effects:
Recovering from such a catastrophic event would take a considerable amount of time. The immediate aftermath would be marked by widespread devastation and loss of life. Over time, the Earth would gradually heal, with ecosystems adapting and recovering, but the process could take millions of years.

It is important to note that the likelihood of a catastrophic impact on Earth is relatively low, and extensive efforts are in place to detect and track near-Earth objects to mitigate potential risks. However, understanding the consequences of such events allows us to develop strategies for planetary defense and take proactive measures to safeguard our planet and its ecosystems.

## Science as a means to Disarmament

The equation $E = mc^2$ is one of the most famous and important equations in physics. It relates energy (E) to mass (m) and the speed of light in a vacuum (c). Let's break down the equation and explore its meaning in detail.

E represents energy. In physics, energy refers to the ability to do work or cause a change. It exists in various forms, such as kinetic energy, potential energy, thermal energy, and electromagnetic energy.

M represents mass. Mass is a fundamental property of matter and refers to the amount of material present in an object. It determines the object's inertia and gravitational interaction with other objects.

C represents the speed of light in a vacuum, which is approximately 299,792,458 meters per second. The speed of light is a fundamental constant in the universe and plays a crucial role in the theory of special relativity.

The equation states that the energy (E) of an object is equal to its mass (m) times the speed of light squared ($c^2$). When considering this equation, there are a few important concepts to understand:

1 Energy-Mass Equivalence:
The equation reveals that mass and energy are interchangeable. It suggests that mass can be converted into energy and vice versa. This concept is a fundamental tenet of Einstein's theory of relativity.

2 Enormous Amounts of Energy:
The equation highlights that even a small amount of mass can contain a significant amount of energy. The speed of light squared ($c^2$) is an enormous value, which means that a small amount of mass can yield a large amount of energy. This principle is the basis for nuclear reactions, where a small amount of mass is converted into a tremendous amount of energy.

3 Speed of Light as an Upper Limit:
The equation also implies that nothing with mass can travel at or exceed the speed of light. As an object approaches the speed of light, its energy and momentum increase dramatically, and it requires an infinite amount of energy to accelerate it to the speed of light.

Einstein's equation $E = mc^2$ revolutionized our understanding of energy, mass, and the relationship between the two. It has profound implications in various fields of physics, including particle physics, nuclear energy, and cosmology. The equation has been verified by numerous experiments and observations, and its accuracy has been confirmed in various contexts.

Relativity, specifically the theory of special relativity developed by Albert Einstein, does not directly define or describe peace. The theory of special relativity is a physical theory that revolutionized our understanding of space, time, and the relationship between matter and energy. However, we can explore a philosophical interpretation of peace within the context of relativity.

Relativity teaches us that space and time are intertwined and that they are not absolute, but rather depend on the relative motion of observers. It emphasizes that there is no preferred frame of reference, and the laws of physics hold true regardless of an observer's motion. This principle challenges the notion of an absolute, fixed perspective and encourages a broader, more inclusive understanding of reality. In the context of peace, we can draw an analogy from relativity. Just as relativity promotes the idea of multiple valid perspectives, peace can be seen as a state where diverse individuals, communities, and nations coexist harmoniously, respecting and valuing each other's perspectives, rights, and dignity.

Relativity also highlights the interconnectedness of the universe. It suggests that all matter and energy are connected through a complex web of interactions. Similarly, peace can be seen as recognizing and nurturing the interconnectedness of humanity, fostering cooperation, understanding, and empathy among individuals and nations. Moreover, relativity emphasizes that the laws of physics are consistent across different frames of reference. In the context of peace, this can be interpreted as the universality of principles and values that promote peace, such as justice, equality, compassion, and non-violence. These principles should apply consistently to all individuals and societies, transcending cultural, religious, and national boundaries. While relativity itself does not provide a direct definition of peace, it offers perspectives that can inspire a broader understanding of peace as a state of inclusive coexistence, interconnectedness, and adherence to universal principles. Peace, in this context, encompasses harmony, justice, respect, and the pursuit of shared well-being for all.

The Heisenberg Uncertainty Principle, formulated by Werner Heisenberg, is a fundamental principle in quantum mechanics. It states that certain pairs of physical properties, such as position and momentum or energy and time, cannot be precisely known or measured simultaneously with arbitrary accuracy. The more precisely one of these properties is known, the less precisely the other can be determined. This principle introduces inherent uncertainty and indeterminacy at the microscopic scale. In the context of life and death, the Heisenberg Uncertainty Principle implies that at the quantum level, the properties and behaviors of fundamental particles, which make up all matter, are inherently uncertain. This uncertainty challenges the notion of a strictly deterministic universe and raises questions about the nature of life and consciousness.

Erwin Schrödinger, one of the pioneers of quantum mechanics, contributed significantly to our understanding of wave mechanics and quantum theory. In

1935, Schrödinger proposed a thought experiment known as "Schrödinger's cat" to illustrate the paradoxical nature of quantum superposition. The experiment involves a cat enclosed in a box with a radioactive source that may or may not trigger the release of a poison, based on the decay of a radioactive atom. According to quantum mechanics, until the box is opened and observed, the cat exists in a superposition of both being alive and dead simultaneously. This highlights the concept of quantum states and the peculiar nature of reality at the quantum level.

J. Robert Oppenheimer, one of the key scientists involved in the development of the atomic bomb, pondered philosophical questions related to life and death. He was influenced by Eastern philosophical ideas, particularly from Hinduism and the Bhagavad Gita. Oppenheimer famously quoted the Bhagavad Gita upon witnessing the first atomic bomb explosion: "Now I am become Death, the destroyer of worlds." His quote reflects a deep contemplation on the profound impact of human actions and the complex ethical implications of scientific discoveries. From Oppenheimer's perspective, the concepts of life and death are intimately connected, and the power of scientific advancements can have far-reaching consequences. Quantum mechanics, with its probabilistic and uncertain nature, challenges the traditional notions of deterministic cause-and-effect relationships and the distinction between life and death as discrete states. It raises philosophical questions about the nature of reality and our place within it.

The Heisenberg Uncertainty Principle introduces inherent uncertainty at the quantum level, challenging deterministic views of the universe. Schrödinger's cat experiment highlights the concept of quantum superposition, where quantum states can exist in multiple possibilities simultaneously. Oppenheimer's contemplation on life and death reflects a profound recognition of the ethical and philosophical implications of scientific discoveries. Quantum mechanics opens up avenues for philosophical reflections on the interconnectedness and relative nature of life and death, inviting us to explore the profound mysteries of existence.

**And so to the Alcubierre Drive..**

Designing a hypothetical Alcubierre drive that remains as feasible as possible requires considering the current scientific understanding and addressing the major challenges associated with the concept. Please note that while the Alcubierre drive is a theoretical concept within the realm of general relativity, there are significant technological and theoretical obstacles that make its practical realisation highly speculative at this point. Nonetheless, here is a hypothetical design for an Alcubierre drive:

1. Warp Bubble Generation:
The Alcubierre drive would require the generation of a warp bubble, a region of manipulated spacetime around the spacecraft. This bubble would contract space in front of the spacecraft and expand space behind it. This contraction and expansion of spacetime would create a "warp drive" effect, allowing the spacecraft to travel faster than the speed of light locally.

2. Exotic Matter:
The Alcubierre drive concept proposes the use of "exotic matter" with negative energy density to achieve the necessary manipulation of spacetime. This exotic matter would need to possess properties not currently known or understood in our current understanding of physics. The challenge lies in finding or creating such exotic matter and understanding how to manipulate it effectively.

3. Energy Requirements:
The energy requirements for an Alcubierre drive are immense. The drive would need to generate enormous amounts of negative energy to create and sustain the warp bubble. It would require a highly advanced and efficient energy source, possibly utilizing exotic forms of energy or harnessing the power of quantum phenomena.

4. Control and Navigation:
Precise control and navigation within the warp bubble would be essential. The spacecraft would need mechanisms to modulate the warp bubble's size, shape, and intensity, allowing for maneuverability and course corrections. This would require advanced propulsion and navigation systems capable of adjusting the spacetime curvature in real-time.

5. Safety Considerations:
The Alcubierre drive could potentially encounter hazards during operation, such as gravitational waves, high-energy particles, or interactions with the surrounding spacetime. Robust shielding and protective measures would be necessary to ensure the safety of the spacecraft and its occupants during travel.

6. Ethical and Regulatory Concerns:
The development and deployment of an Alcubierre drive would raise various ethical and regulatory questions. Considerations related to environmental impacts, potential disruptions to spacetime, and the consequences of faster-than-light travel on causality and relativity principles would need to be addressed.

It is crucial to emphasize that the feasibility of an Alcubierre drive is highly speculative and currently beyond our scientific capabilities. The design provided here is based on theoretical concepts and assumptions, but practical implementation would require significant advancements in our understanding of physics, energy manipulation, and exotic matter. Ongoing scientific research and technological breakthroughs will be essential for exploring the feasibility and potential of such a propulsion system.

**String theory to M theory**

String theory is a theoretical framework that seeks to describe the fundamental building blocks of the universe as tiny, vibrating strings. While it is a complex and ongoing area of research, it has not yet been fully solved. However, I can provide an overview of string theory and its main concepts. String theory suggests that elementary particles such as electrons and quarks are not point-like particles but rather tiny strings, similar to violin strings. These strings vibrate at different frequencies, giving rise to different particle types and their properties, including mass and charge. The theory also proposes additional spatial dimensions beyond the familiar three dimensions of space and one dimension of time.

There are different versions of string theory, such as Type I, Type IIA, Type IIB, heterotic SO(32), and heterotic E8×E8. These versions vary in their mathematical structures and the number of dimensions they require. For example, some versions require ten dimensions, while others may require eleven dimensions. One of the major challenges in string theory is the issue of quantisation, which is the process of applying the principles of quantum mechanics to the theory. In quantum mechanics, particles are described by wave functions that represent the probabilities of different outcomes. However, in string theory, the equations describing the behavior of strings are more complex, and a complete and consistent formulation of quantum string theory is still being sought.

Another challenge is the existence of different solutions or configurations of string theory known as "string vacua." These different solutions correspond to different possible universes with different physical laws and properties. The challenge is to identify which solution corresponds to our observed universe and to explain why the others are not realized. Furthermore, string theory has connections to other areas of physics, such as general relativity and quantum field theory, and it attempts to provide a unified framework that encompasses all known fundamental forces and particles. However, reconciling string theory with these other theories, particularly with gravity, is an ongoing challenge.

In summary, while string theory offers a promising framework for understanding the fundamental nature of the universe, it remains an active area of research with many unresolved questions. Scientists continue to work towards finding a complete and consistent formulation of the theory and exploring its implications for our understanding of the cosmos.

M-theory, also known as the mother of all theories, is a proposed extension of string theory that attempts to unify different versions of string theory and incorporate other theories, such as supergravity and 11-dimensional supergravity. While M-theory is a subject of ongoing research and is not yet fully understood or solved, I can provide an overview of its key concepts. M-theory suggests that the fundamental building blocks of the universe are not just one-dimensional strings but extended objects called membranes or branes. These branes can have different dimensions, such as zero-dimensional particles (point-like objects), one-dimensional strings, two-dimensional membranes, and so on. One of the significant features of M-theory is its inclusion of higher-dimensional objects. In addition to the familiar four dimensions of spacetime (three spatial dimensions and one time dimension), M-theory requires the existence of additional spatial dimensions. The specific number of dimensions varies depending on the version of M-theory being considered, but the most commonly studied version involves 11 dimensions. The existence of these extra dimensions provides a means to unify the fundamental forces of nature, including gravity, electromagnetism, and the strong and weak nuclear forces. M-theory suggests that these forces are different manifestations of a more fundamental underlying theory. However, solving M-theory poses significant challenges. The theory lacks a complete formulation and equations that fully describe its dynamics. Additionally, the vast number of possible solutions, known as the "landscape" of M-theory, makes it difficult to identify which solution corresponds to our observed universe.

Furthermore, M-theory also raises questions about the nature of spacetime and the geometry of the extra dimensions. The theory suggests that these dimensions may be compactified or curled up into tiny, nearly imperceptible shapes, which has implications for the behaviour of particles and the scale at which gravity becomes significant. Despite these challenges, M-theory has provided valuable insights into the nature of fundamental physics and the potential for a unified theory of everything. Researchers continue to explore its mathematical and conceptual foundations, seeking a complete understanding of its principles and implications for our understanding of the universe.

In summary, M-theory is a proposed framework that extends string theory and aims to unify the fundamental forces of nature. While it remains an active area of research and is not yet fully solved, it offers promising avenues for investigating the nature of the universe at its most fundamental level.

String theory and M-theory are related in the sense that M-theory can be seen as a unifying framework that encompasses different versions of string theory. While there isn't a fully established mathematical bridge between the two, there are connections and relationships that have been explored by researchers. Here are a few ways in which string theory and M-theory can be linked mathematically:

1. Duality: String theory exhibits a remarkable property known as duality, which relates seemingly different physical theories. For example, there is a duality known as T-duality that relates string theories compactified on small circles of different radii. Another example is the AdS/CFT correspondence, which relates string theory in an anti-de Sitter (AdS) space to a conformal field theory (CFT) on its boundary. These dualities can be seen as mathematical bridges between different string theories and M-theory, providing equivalent descriptions of the same physical phenomena.

2. Supergravity: M-theory includes eleven-dimensional supergravity as a low-energy limit. Supergravity is a supersymmetric theory of gravity that incorporates supersymmetry and describes the interactions of gravitons, gauge fields, and matter particles. String theory also includes supergravity in its low-energy limit, and in certain cases, it can be seen as a perturbative expansion of M-theory. The mathematical framework of supergravity provides a link between string theory and M-theory.

3. Branes and Extended Objects: M-theory introduces extended objects called branes, which include not only one-dimensional strings but also higher-dimensional membranes. String theory can be seen as a special case of M-theory when the membranes are not considered. The mathematical description of branes and their interactions in M-theory provides a connection to the fundamental strings of string theory.

4. Mathematical Structures: Both string theory and M-theory rely on sophisticated mathematical structures. These include concepts from differential geometry, algebraic geometry, topology, and group theory. Mathematical techniques such as conformal field theory, algebraic K-theory, and homological algebra have been used to study various aspects of string theory and M-theory. The shared mathematical foundations allow for potential connections and relationships between the two theories.

## The Many-Worlds Interpretation

The Many-Worlds Interpretation (MWI) is a theoretical framework in quantum mechanics that proposes the existence of multiple parallel universes or "worlds." It was first introduced by physicist Hugh Everett in the 1950s as a way to address the measurement problem and the nature of quantum superposition. The core idea of the Many-Worlds Interpretation is that every time a quantum measurement or observation occurs, the universe branches into multiple non-interacting parallel universes, each representing a different possible outcome of the measurement. In other words, instead of the collapse of the wavefunction that occurs in other interpretations of quantum mechanics, MWI suggests that all possible outcomes of a measurement actually occur in separate universes.

Key Elements of Many-Worlds Interpretation:

1. Superposition: According to MWI, quantum systems can exist in superposition states, where they simultaneously exist in multiple states or configurations. For example, a particle can be in a superposition of being in two different locations or having multiple energy states.

2. Branching Universes: When a measurement or observation is made on a quantum system, the universe splits into multiple branches, each corresponding to a different outcome of the measurement. Each branch represents a separate universe with a different set of physical properties and states.

3. Parallel Universes: These branches or parallel universes are separate and non-interacting, meaning that information and events in one universe do not influence or affect events in another. Each universe follows its own distinct set of physical laws and evolves independently.

4. Probability and Determinism: MWI maintains that probabilities in quantum mechanics arise from the subjective knowledge and uncertainty of an observer rather than objective randomness. In each branch, all possible outcomes of a measurement occur with a certain probability, reflecting the observer's limited knowledge of which branch they are in.

5. Universal Wavefunction: MWI describes the entire physical universe as a single wavefunction that encompasses all possible states and configurations. Each branch represents a specific term or component of the wavefunction, and the evolution of the wavefunction is governed by the Schrödinger equation.

Criticism and Interpretation:

The Many-Worlds Interpretation is a controversial interpretation of quantum mechanics, and it is not universally accepted among physicists. Some criticisms and alternative interpretations include:

- Complexity and Occam's Razor: Critics argue that MWI introduces an enormous number of parallel universes, raising questions about the simplicity and explanatory power of the theory compared to other interpretations.

- Observer's Role: The role of consciousness and observation in the branching of universes is a topic of debate. Some argue that the observer's conscious experience can only exist in one universe, leading to questions about the nature of subjective experience and its relation to branching universes.

- Experimental Verification: Due to the inherent difficulty of directly observing or testing the existence of parallel universes, MWI remains a theoretical framework without conclusive experimental evidence.

Despite these challenges and criticisms, the Many-Worlds Interpretation continues to be a thought-provoking and actively researched area within the field of quantum mechanics, providing a unique perspective on the nature of reality, superposition, and the possibilities of multiple parallel universes.

## Future, Past and Present

The future is a concept that refers to the period of time that is yet to come. It encompasses the events, circumstances, and developments that lie ahead, extending beyond the present moment. While the future is inherently uncertain and cannot be predicted with absolute certainty, humans have a natural curiosity and desire to understand and anticipate what lies ahead.

1. Theoretical Perspectives on the Future:
 - Determinism: Some philosophical and scientific perspectives suggest that the future is predetermined by a chain of cause and effect, following deterministic laws. According to this view, the future is already fixed and can be theoretically determined if one possesses complete knowledge of the present.

 - Probabilistic or Stochastic Views: In many fields, including quantum mechanics, economics, and weather forecasting, the future is considered probabilistic rather than deterministic. These perspectives recognize that there are inherent uncertainties and probabilities associated with future events. Prediction and forecasting involve estimating likely outcomes based on available data and statistical models.

 - Open Future: From a philosophical perspective, some argue that the future remains open and indeterminate. This view emphasizes human agency and the power of choices and actions to shape the course of events. According to this perspective, the future is not predetermined but emerges through the interplay of individual and collective decisions and actions.

2. Anticipation and Planning:
Humans have a natural tendency to anticipate and plan for the future. This ability sets us apart from other animals and enables us to consider possible scenarios, set goals, and take steps to achieve them. Planning for the future involves assessing risks, identifying opportunities, and making decisions based on available information and desired outcomes.

3. Technological Advancements:
The future is often closely associated with technological advancements and their potential impacts on various aspects of human life. Technological progress has shaped human civilization throughout history, and it is likely to continue doing so in the future. Innovations in fields such as artificial intelligence, biotechnology, space exploration, renewable energy, and communication have the potential to bring significant changes to society and shape the future.

4. Uncertainty and Complexity:
The future is inherently uncertain and influenced by numerous factors, including social, economic, environmental, and political dynamics. Complex systems, such as global economies or ecosystems, exhibit non-linear behavior, making accurate predictions challenging. Additionally, unforeseen events, known as "black swan" events, can have profound and unpredictable impacts on the future.

5. Human Agency and Responsibility:
As active participants in shaping the future, humans have a responsibility to consider the long-term consequences of their actions and decisions. This includes addressing global challenges such as climate change, resource depletion, inequality, and technological risks. Collective efforts, collaboration, and responsible decision-making are crucial for creating a more sustainable and desirable future.

It is important to note that while we can speculate, theorize, and plan for the future, the actual unfolding of events will always be subject to a multitude of unpredictable factors. Therefore, a balanced perspective involves embracing uncertainty, adapting to change, and fostering resilience to navigate the complexities of an ever-evolving future.

The past refers to the period of time that has already occurred, encompassing events, experiences, and phenomena that have happened prior to the present moment. It represents a recorded history of human civilization and the natural world. While the past cannot be changed or directly observed, it is an essential aspect of human understanding and knowledge.

1. Definition and Study of the Past:

The past is typically studied through various disciplines, including history, archaeology, paleontology, anthropology, and other branches of social sciences and natural sciences. These fields employ different methodologies, such as analyzing written records, excavating artifacts, studying fossils, and reconstructing past societies and environments.

2. Historical Perspective:

The past provides a historical perspective that helps us understand the origins, development, and progression of human civilization, cultures, and societies. It includes the exploration of significant events, individuals, social movements, wars, technological advancements, and cultural shifts that have shaped our present reality.

3. Preservation and Documentation:

The preservation and documentation of the past are crucial in order to maintain a record of human achievements, cultural heritage, and scientific discoveries. Written records, oral traditions, archaeological sites, artifacts, photographs, and other forms of documentation provide valuable insights into past civilizations and allow us to study and learn from them.

4. Interpretation and Understanding:

The past is subject to interpretation and understanding, as historical accounts can be influenced by biases, perspectives, and the availability of evidence. Historians and researchers analyze primary and secondary sources, apply critical thinking, and engage in scholarly debates to construct narratives and interpretations of the past.

5. Impact on the Present:

The past has a significant impact on the present. It shapes our identities, cultural heritage, societal norms, and systems of governance. Lessons learned from the past can inform decision-making, policies, and social progress. Additionally, the study of history can help us avoid repeating past mistakes and promote a more inclusive and just society.

6. Historical Memory and Collective Identity:

The past is an integral part of individual and collective memory, influencing cultural identities and shared narratives. It contributes to the formation of national, ethnic, and communal identities, as well as personal and familial histories. Remembering and commemorating historical events can shape societal values, traditions, and intergenerational connections.

7. Theoretical Approaches:
Theoretical frameworks, such as historiography and historical theory, provide perspectives and methods for analyzing the past. These approaches include examining primary sources, considering different historical interpretations, understanding the context of events, and exploring the role of individuals, structures, and societal forces in shaping history.

While the past itself is fixed and unchangeable, our understanding of it is constantly evolving as new evidence is discovered and interpretations are refined. The study of the past helps us gain insights into human experiences, societal developments, and the forces that have shaped our world, ultimately contributing to a deeper understanding of our present reality.

The present, from a general parallax perspective influenced by relativity, refers to the "now" moment that is experienced by an observer at a particular point in space and time. Relativity, particularly special relativity, provides insights into the nature of the present and its relationship to the observer's frame of reference.

1. Definition of the Present:
The present is the instant in time that is perceived as "now." It represents the immediate moment in which events and experiences occur. It is the point at which past events transition into the future.

2. Relativity and the Observer's Frame of Reference:
According to the theory of relativity, the perception of the present can vary depending on the observer's motion and relative position in space. This is known as the relativity of simultaneity. Different observers moving at different speeds or occupying different locations may experience events occurring at different times.

3. Time Dilation and the Present:
Special relativity also introduces the concept of time dilation, which suggests that time can pass at different rates for observers in relative motion. As an observer's velocity approaches the speed of light, time appears to slow down from the perspective of a stationary observer. This implies that the present moment can differ between observers with different velocities.

4. Spacetime and the Present:
In the framework of relativity, spacetime is a unified four-dimensional continuum that combines three dimensions of space with one dimension of time. The present is seen as a "slice" of this four-dimensional spacetime. The relativi-

ty of simultaneity implies that different observers moving at different velocities may slice spacetime differently, perceiving events at different moments as their present.

5. Parallax Perspectives and the Present:
Parallax refers to the apparent shift or difference in the position or direction of an object when viewed from different vantage points. In the context of relativity, parallax perspectives arise due to the relative motion and spatial separation of observers. This can lead to differences in the perception of the present moment and the order of events.

6. Theoretical Implications and Perspectives:
The relativity of the present challenges the idea of an absolute "now" that is universally experienced by all observers. Instead, it suggests that the present is a relative concept, dependent on an observer's frame of reference and their relationship to the events and objects being observed.

7. Philosophical Considerations:
The relativity of the present raises philosophical questions about the nature of time, the subjective experience of the present moment, and the distinction between past, present, and future. It invites contemplation on the relationship between perception, reality, and the observer's role in shaping their experience of the present.

It's important to note that while relativity provides a theoretical framework for understanding the present from a parallax perspective, its effects are typically negligible in everyday life situations. For practical purposes, a universal present moment is often assumed, allowing for synchronized human activities and shared experiences.

**Creating a new dimension (e.g. time)**

Creating a new dimension is a concept that goes beyond our current scientific understanding and technological capabilities. In the realm of physics, dimensions are fundamental properties of space and time that define the coordinates and directions in which objects and events can exist and occur. Our universe is commonly described as having three spatial dimensions (length, width, and height) and one temporal dimension (time). However, speculative theories, such as string theory or certain branches of quantum physics, propose the existence of additional dimensions beyond the ones we can directly perceive. These extra dimensions are thought to be compacted or curled up at incredibly small scales, making them unobservable in our everyday experiences.

While theories and mathematics can describe the possibility of additional dimensions, creating or accessing new dimensions is currently beyond our capabilities. The physical properties and existence of dimensions are deeply intertwined with the fundamental laws of nature, and altering or creating dimensions would require a profound understanding and manipulation of these laws. In order to contemplate the creation of a new dimension, one would need to consider advancements in our understanding of physics, potentially including unified theories that reconcile quantum mechanics and general relativity. Additionally, the technological means to manipulate space-time at a fundamental level would need to be developed, surpassing our current limitations.

It's important to note that the creation of a new dimension is purely speculative and hypothetical at this point. It represents a topic of active research and theoretical exploration within the scientific community, but practical realization or creation of new dimensions remains firmly in the realm of scientific imagination and discovery.

**<u>Faster Than Light travel (FTL)</u>**

Faster-than-light (FTL) travel, as currently understood, presents significant challenges based on our current scientific understanding. The theory of relativity, developed by Albert Einstein, places limitations on the speed at which information, matter, and energy can travel through space. According to our current knowledge, it is not possible for any object or information to exceed the speed of light in a vacuum (299,792,458 meters per second).

If FTL travel were to be achieved, it would require groundbreaking advances in physics and a deep rethinking of our understanding of space, time, and energy. Here are some of the key considerations and challenges associated with FTL travel:

1. Warp Drives and Wormholes:
Theoretical concepts such as warp drives and wormholes have been proposed as potential means for achieving FTL travel. Warp drives involve manipulating spacetime to create a "warp bubble" that allows a spacecraft to traverse space at speeds greater than light. Wormholes are hypothetical tunnels connecting different regions of spacetime that could potentially provide shortcuts for travel. However, both concepts rely on exotic and speculative physics, such as negative energy densities or traversable wormholes, which have not been observed or confirmed.

2. Energy Requirements:
FTL travel would likely require enormous amounts of energy. The energy needed to surpass the speed of light, based on our current understanding, would be

staggering. Harnessing such energy and finding ways to generate and control it would be a monumental technological and scientific challenge.

3. Time Dilation and Paradoxes:
According to the theory of relativity, as an object approaches the speed of light, time dilation occurs. Time passes more slowly for objects in motion relative to a stationary observer. This phenomenon raises questions and paradoxes when it comes to FTL travel, including the potential for time travel or causality violations. Resolving these paradoxes and understanding the consequences of FTL travel on the fabric of space and time is a complex task.

4. Human Effects:
The effects of FTL travel on humans are speculative and largely unknown. The extreme speeds and potential manipulation of spacetime could subject travelers to significant forces, accelerations, and gravitational distortions. Understanding the impact of such conditions on the human body, including physiological and psychological effects, would require extensive research and testing.

It's important to recognize that FTL travel remains highly speculative and theoretical within the current scientific framework. While it is an exciting topic for science fiction and imagination, achieving FTL travel would require revolutionary breakthroughs in our understanding of physics, energy, and spacetime. Additionally, understanding the potential effects on humans would require advanced knowledge of human physiology, adaptability, and engineering to ensure the safety and well-being of space travelers.

**Robotic Technology and space investment**

Investing in robotic technology for space exploration and mining purposes can be a strategic and promising endeavor. Here are some reasons why it could be considered a smart investment:

1 Efficiency and Precision: Robotic systems can be designed to perform tasks with high precision and accuracy, eliminating human error. They can work tirelessly and consistently, reducing the risk of accidents and improving overall efficiency. Robotic exploration and mining missions can gather data, analyze samples, and carry out complex operations in harsh and remote environments more effectively than human counterparts.

2 Cost-Effectiveness: Sending humans to space involves numerous challenges, including life support systems, safety measures, and the need for

return missions. Robotic missions can be more cost-effective since they eliminate many of these requirements and can be designed for specific tasks. Additionally, robotic systems can be reusable or easily replaceable, reducing overall costs.

3 Risk Mitigation: Space exploration and mining involve inherent risks, such as exposure to radiation, extreme temperatures, and the unknown nature of space environments. Deploying robots instead of humans reduces the potential risks to human life and allows for more exploratory and experimental missions without endangering human lives.

4 Adaptability and Versatility: Robotic systems can be designed and programmed to adapt to different scenarios and environments. They can be upgraded, reconfigured, or repurposed for various missions, making them versatile tools for space exploration and mining. This adaptability allows for a wider range of missions and enables continuous technological advancements.

5 Long-Term Operations: Robotic systems can be designed to withstand extended periods in space or on other celestial bodies, where human presence is impractical or unfeasible. They can continue operations for extended durations, providing valuable data and insights over time.

6 Scientific Discoveries: Robotic missions have been instrumental in making significant scientific discoveries and advancing our understanding of the universe. They can collect samples, analyze geological formations, study celestial bodies, and conduct experiments in ways that greatly contribute to scientific knowledge.

However, it is important to strike a balance between robotic missions and human presence in space exploration and mining. Human astronauts offer unique capabilities such as adaptability, decision-making skills, and the ability to handle unexpected situations. Therefore, a combination of robotic systems and human exploration can maximize the benefits and potential of space missions.

Overall, investing in robotic technology for space exploration and mining has the potential to yield valuable scientific, economic, and technological outcomes. It can expand our knowledge of the cosmos, facilitate resource utilization, and pave the way for future human endeavors in space.

**Black Holes and White Holes**

A white hole and a black hole are both hypothetical astronomical objects, but they possess contrasting characteristics and behaviors. Here's a definition and explanation of the differences between the two:

Black Hole:
A black hole is a region in space where the gravitational pull is so strong that nothing, not even light, can escape its gravitational field. It forms from the remnants of massive stars that have undergone gravitational collapse. The key features of a black hole include:

1. Event Horizon: The boundary surrounding a black hole beyond which nothing can escape its gravitational pull. Once an object crosses the event horizon, it is believed to be irretrievably drawn into the black hole.

2. Singularity: At the center of a black hole, there is a point of infinite density and space-time curvature called a singularity. The laws of physics, as we currently understand them, break down at this point.

3. Strong Gravitational Pull: Black holes have an immense gravitational force that bends space and time around them, creating a gravitational well from which nothing can escape.

White Hole:
A white hole is a hypothetical region in space that is the opposite of a black hole. Instead of objects and light being pulled inward, a white hole is postulated to be a region from which matter, energy, or information can only emerge and not enter. Some theoretical physicists have proposed the concept of white holes as a consequence of the mathematical equations of general relativity, but no definitive evidence of their existence has been found. The key features of a white hole include:

1. No Event Horizon: Unlike a black hole, a white hole is theorized to have no event horizon. Instead, it would have a reverse event horizon, through which nothing can enter, but from which matter and energy could emerge.

2. Ejection of Matter: It is postulated that a white hole would expel matter, energy, or other forms of radiation outward, potentially creating a flow of particles moving away from the white hole.

3. Time Reversal: The concept of a white hole has been linked to time reversal, suggesting that the arrow of time may flow in the opposite direction compared to our normal experience.

4. Speculative Nature: While black holes have some observational evidence supporting their existence, white holes are purely hypothetical constructs derived from mathematical models.

In summary, a black hole is a region in space from which nothing can escape, including light, due to its intense gravitational pull. A white hole, on the other hand, is a hypothetical region theorized to be the opposite of a black hole, where matter, energy, or information can only emerge and not enter.

***The following concept proposed involves reimagining the birth of the universe based on the presence of white holes and theorized black holes, with a collapse of all stars leading to a singular point, and challenging the traditional understanding of the Big Bang. While this idea is intriguing, it is important to note that it deviates from the current scientific consensus and poses several challenges.***

White holes, as hypothetical astronomical objects, are theorized to be regions from which matter, energy, or information can only emerge and not enter. In your hypothesis, you suggest that the present moment could be the birth of the universe, with the emergence of matter and energy from a white hole. However, white holes have not been observed or confirmed, and their existence remains speculative within the framework of general relativity. Additionally, the concept of a collapse of all stars to a singular point contradicts our understanding of black holes. Black holes are formed from massive stars undergoing gravitational collapse, resulting in a singularity, a point of infinite density at their core. While black holes possess immense gravitational pull, they are not typically associated with the collapse of all stars into a single point. Rather, they are individual objects with their own unique characteristics.

In terms of mathematical evidence, it is challenging to provide definitive mathematical support for a hypothesis that deviates from established models and theories. Mathematics in physics plays a crucial role in formulating and testing theories, but it relies on empirical observations, experimental data, and theoretical consistency. As of now, the prevailing scientific consensus is rooted in the Big Bang theory, which provides a comprehensive explanation for the early universe's expansion and subsequent cosmic evolution.

While it is important to explore alternative ideas and push the boundaries of scientific understanding, it is necessary to critically evaluate and substantiate them with empirical evidence and rigorous mathematical frameworks. The proposed hypothesis involving white holes and the collapse of all stars to a singular point requires significant theoretical development, observational evidence, and validation within the framework of modern physics.

The origin of the universe and how it started is a topic of active scientific investigation and inquiry. The prevailing scientific framework for understanding the origin of the universe is the Big Bang theory. According to this theory, the universe began approximately 13.8 billion years ago in a hot, dense, and rapidly expanding state. While the exact details of the initial moments of the universe's existence are still being explored, I can provide an overview of the mathematical evidence supporting the Big Bang theory.

The mathematical evidence supporting the Big Bang theory is based on several key pillars:

1 Hubble's Law and the Expansion of the Universe:
In the 1920s, astronomer Edwin Hubble observed that distant galaxies are moving away from us, and their recession velocities are proportional to their distances. This relationship, known as Hubble's Law, provides empirical evidence for the expansion of the universe. The mathematical framework describing this expansion is derived from Einstein's general theory of relativity.

2 Cosmic Microwave Background Radiation (CMB):
In the 1960s, the discovery of the cosmic microwave background radiation provided strong evidence for the Big Bang theory. This radiation is a remnant from the early stages of the universe when it transitioned from an opaque, hot plasma to a transparent, cool state. The CMB exhibits a nearly uniform distribution across the sky and has a characteristic temperature that matches the predictions of the Big Bang model.

3 Nucleosynthesis:
The abundance of light elements, such as hydrogen and helium, in the universe is another piece of mathematical evidence supporting the Big Bang theory. The primordial nucleosynthesis that occurred during the first few minutes after the Big Bang predicts the observed ratios of these elements. The calculations involving nuclear reactions and the physics of particle interactions successfully match the observed abundances.

4 Cosmic Large-Scale Structure:
Observations of the large-scale structure of the universe, including galaxy clusters, filaments, and voids, provide further support for the Big Bang theory. Mathematical models based on the theory of gravitational instability and the

growth of density fluctuations accurately reproduce the observed distribution of matter in the universe.

It is important to note that while these mathematical pieces of evidence strongly support the Big Bang theory, they do not provide a complete understanding of the initial singularity or the exact mechanisms that triggered the Big Bang itself. The universe's earliest moments are currently beyond the reach of our observational and mathematical tools, and more research is needed to gain deeper insights into the origin of the universe.

In summary, the mathematical evidence supporting the Big Bang theory is derived from observations of the universe's expansion, the cosmic microwave background radiation, nucleosynthesis calculations, and the large-scale structure of the cosmos. These mathematical frameworks, along with empirical evidence, provide a compelling understanding of the universe's origin and its subsequent evolution.

There are several known types of stars based on their characteristics, including size, temperature, and spectral features. Here are some of the main types of stars:

1. Main Sequence Stars: The majority of stars, including our Sun, fall into this category. They fuse hydrogen into helium in their cores and follow a stable and balanced path on the Hertzsprung-Russell diagram, which plots stars' luminosity against their surface temperature.

2. Red Giants: Red giants are evolved stars that have exhausted their core hydrogen fuel. They have expanded and cooled, causing their outer layers to become red in color. Red giants can vary in size, with some being hundreds of times larger than the Sun.

3. White Dwarfs: White dwarfs are the remnants of low- to medium-mass stars that have exhausted their nuclear fuel. They are incredibly dense and typically have a size comparable to that of Earth but with a mass similar to the Sun. White dwarfs gradually cool and fade over billions of years.

4. Blue Giants/Supergiants: Blue giants and supergiants are massive, hot stars with luminosities that surpass those of main sequence stars by a significant margin. They emit a large amount of ultraviolet radiation and have relatively short lifespans compared to other types of stars.

5. Neutron Stars: Neutron stars are extremely dense stellar remnants that form after the collapse of massive stars in supernova explosions. They are composed primarily of neutrons and have extremely strong gravitational and magnetic

fields. Neutron stars can rotate rapidly, emitting beams of radiation that are observable as pulsars.

6. Black Holes: Black holes are formed when massive stars collapse under their own gravity, creating an incredibly dense region from which nothing, not even light, can escape. Their gravitational pull is so intense that they warp spacetime around them. Black holes are currently only detectable through their gravitational effects on nearby matter.

These are just a few examples of the known types of stars, and there is a wide variety of variations and subclasses within each category. The classification and study of stars continue to be an active area of research, with new discoveries and refinements to our understanding regularly occurring.

Stars can be classified into different types and classes based on their characteristics, primarily their spectral properties, luminosity, temperature, and size. Here is a comprehensive breakdown of the types and classes of stars:

1. O-Type Stars:
   - These are extremely hot and massive stars.
   - They have blue-white color and high surface temperatures.
   - O-type stars are rare and among the most luminous stars in the universe.

2. B-Type Stars:
   - B-type stars are also hot and massive, but slightly cooler than O-type stars.
   - They have a blue-white color.
   - B-type stars exhibit prominent absorption lines of helium in their spectra.

3. A-Type Stars:
   - A-type stars are hot and relatively bright.
   - They have a white or bluish-white color.
   - These stars show strong hydrogen spectral lines and moderate metal lines.

4. F-Type Stars:
   - F-type stars are slightly cooler than A-type stars.
   - They have a white or yellow-white color.
   - F-type stars exhibit weaker hydrogen lines but stronger ionized calcium lines.

5. G-Type Stars:
   - G-type stars include our Sun (G2V).
   - They have a yellow color.

- G-type stars are relatively stable and serve as a benchmark for comparing other stars.

6. K-Type Stars:
   - K-type stars are cooler and less massive than G-type stars.
   - They have an orange color.
   - These stars exhibit prominent absorption lines of ionized calcium and metal oxides.

7. M-Type Stars:
   - M-type stars are the coolest and most common type of main sequence stars.
   - They have a reddish color.
   - M-type stars have strong absorption bands of molecules like titanium oxide.

8. L-Type Stars:
   - L-type stars are cool and relatively dim.
   - They have a red color.
   - L-type stars have distinctive spectra with metal hydride and alkali metal lines.

9. T-Type Stars:
   - T-type stars are even cooler than L-type stars.
   - They have a reddish color and exhibit methane absorption features in their spectra.
   - T-type stars are often called "methane dwarfs."

10. Y-Type Stars:
   - Y-type stars are the coolest and least luminous known stars.
   - They have a reddish color and exhibit strong absorption lines of ammonia in their spectra.
   - Y-type stars are often referred to as "brown dwarfs."

These classifications, known as spectral classes, are further divided into sub-classes denoted by numeric values (0-9), with 0 indicating the hottest and 9 indicating the coolest within a particular spectral type.

It is important to note that this classification system primarily applies to main sequence stars, and there are other types of stars, such as white dwarfs, neutron stars, and black holes, which have different classification schemes based on their unique characteristics.

Chapter 1: Mining Stars: Extracting Resources from the Cosmos

Mining stars, while a captivating concept, remains beyond our current technological capabilities. Stars are unimaginably massive celestial bodies composed mostly of hydrogen and helium, with nuclear fusion processes occurring at their cores. Extracting resources from stars poses immense challenges due to their extreme conditions and the vast distances that separate us from them.

However, as humanity continues to advance in space exploration and resource utilization, it is crucial to consider potential future technologies that may enable stellar resource extraction. This chapter explores speculative concepts and theoretical frameworks for star mining, including:

1. Stellar Engineering: Hypothetical methods for manipulating the energy output or composition of a star, such as controlled fusion ignition or the introduction of materials to enhance resource availability.

2. Stellar Evolution: Understanding the life cycles of stars, including their birth, fusion processes, and eventual demise, can provide insights into potential opportunities for resource extraction at different stages.

3. Advanced Robotics: Autonomous robotic systems capable of withstanding the extreme conditions near stars could potentially perform mining operations or gather data for scientific analysis.

While star mining is currently in the realm of science fiction, it is valuable to explore these possibilities and stimulate scientific curiosity and discussion. Continued advancements in technology and scientific understanding may pave the way for future exploration and resource utilization beyond our planet.

Chapter 2: Fusion: Unleashing the Power of the Stars

Fusion, the process that powers stars, holds immense potential as a clean and virtually limitless source of energy. This chapter delves into the fascinating world of fusion, exploring its principles and the steps required to create a fusion reactor.

1. Fusion Basics: An introduction to nuclear fusion, the process in which atomic nuclei combine to form heavier elements, releasing a vast amount of energy in the process. The chapter explains the key concepts of temperature, density, and confinement required for successful fusion reactions.

2. Fusion Fuel: Detailing the choice of fuel for fusion reactions, primarily focusing on isotopes of hydrogen, such as deuterium and tritium. The chapter explains their availability, extraction, and the conditions necessary for initiating fusion reactions.

3. Confinement Techniques: Overview of various confinement methods, including magnetic confinement (such as tokamaks and stellarators) and inertial confinement (such as laser or particle beam-driven fusion). The chapter explores the principles behind these techniques and their respective challenges.

4. Ignition and Sustained Fusion: Describing the critical steps required to initiate and sustain fusion reactions, including achieving the necessary temperatures, densities, and confinement timescales. The chapter covers the engineering and scientific challenges associated with creating a self-sustaining fusion reactor.

Chapter 3: Nuclea-Thermo and Quantum Thermo Dynamics: The Science of Energy Conversion

Nuclear thermodynamics and quantum thermodynamics form the foundation for understanding energy conversion processes, including those involved in fusion reactors. This chapter focuses on these fundamental principles and their applications.

1. Nuclea-Thermo Dynamics: Exploring the principles of nuclear thermodynamics, including concepts like energy conservation, entropy, and the laws of thermodynamics. The chapter illustrates how these principles are applicable to nuclear reactions and energy conversion.

2. Quantum Thermo Dynamics: Introducing the intersection of quantum mechanics and thermodynamics, examining the behavior of energy at the quantum level. The chapter explores topics such as energy quantization, statistical mechanics, and the connections between entropy and quantum information.

Chapter 4: Global Disarmament and the Pursuit of Peaceful Technologies

Global disarmament initiatives advocate for the reduction and elimination of nuclear weapons to foster peace and international security. This chapter discusses the importance of global disarmament efforts and the potential for redirecting resources towards the development of peaceful technologies, including fusion energy research. It examines the benefits of promoting international collaboration, scientific exchange, and diplomacy to mitigate nuclear proliferation risks and advance peaceful applications of nuclear science.

By exploring the fascinating realms of star mining, fusion energy, and the underlying principles of nuclear and quantum thermodynamics, we can expand our knowledge and stimulate scientific inquiry towards a sustainable and peaceful future.

Note: This book provides a general outline of the topics and considerations involved. Each chapter can be expanded upon with detailed explanations, scientific data, and specific examples to provide a comprehensive understanding of the subjects covered.

Chapter 1: Mining Stars: Extracting Resources from the Cosmos

Mining Stars: Exploring Future Possibilities
- Introduction to the concept of mining stars and its speculative nature
- Discussion on the challenges posed by extreme conditions and vast distances
- Consideration of potential future technologies for stellar resource extraction
- Exploration of theoretical frameworks, such as stellar engineering and advanced robotics

Chapter 2: Fusion: Unleashing the Power of the Stars

Fusion Basics: A Powerful Energy Source
- Explanation of nuclear fusion as the process powering stars
- Discussion on the fusion of atomic nuclei and energy release
- Introduction to fusion fuels, including deuterium and tritium

Confinement Techniques: Containing the Energy
- Overview of magnetic confinement methods, including tokamaks and stellarators
- Explanation of how magnetic fields control and confine the plasma
- Introduction to inertial confinement methods, such as laser or particle beam-driven fusion

Ignition and Sustained Fusion: Achieving Self-Sustaining Reactions
- Description of the conditions necessary for fusion ignition
- Discussion on the temperature, density, and confinement timescales required
- Exploration of engineering and scientific challenges in creating a self-sustaining fusion reactor

Chapter 3: Nuclea-Thermo and Quantum Thermo Dynamics: The Science of Energy Conversion

Nuclear Thermo Dynamics: Understanding Energy Conversion
- Introduction to the principles of nuclear thermodynamics
- Discussion on energy conservation, entropy, and the laws of thermodynamics
- Illustration of their applicability to nuclear reactions and energy conversion processes

Quantum Thermo Dynamics: Energy at the Quantum Level
- Exploration of the intersection between quantum mechanics and thermodynamics
- Explanation of energy quantization and statistical mechanics
- Discussion on the connections between entropy and quantum information

Chapter 4: Global Disarmament and the Pursuit of Peaceful Technologies

Global Disarmament: Promoting Peace and Security
- Importance of global disarmament initiatives
- Discussion on the reduction and elimination of nuclear weapons
- Exploration of resource redirection towards peaceful technologies

Promoting Peaceful Technologies: Fusion Energy as a Solution
- Advantages of fusion energy as a clean and abundant energy source
- Consideration of international collaboration and scientific exchange
- Examination of the role of diplomacy in mitigating nuclear proliferation risks

Note: Each chapter can be expanded with additional scientific explanations, mathematical derivations, case studies, and real-world examples to provide a comprehensive understanding of the topics covered.

Chapter 1: Mining Stars: Extracting Resources from the Cosmos

Mining Stars: Exploring Future Possibilities
- Introduction to the concept of mining stars and its speculative nature
- Discussion on the challenges posed by extreme conditions and vast distances
- Consideration of potential future technologies for stellar resource extraction
- Exploration of theoretical frameworks, such as stellar engineering and advanced robotics

Stellar Engineering: Manipulating Stars for Resource Extraction

- Hypothetical methods for manipulating the energy output or composition of a star
- Speculation on controlled fusion ignition and potential techniques for enhancing resource availability
- Discussion on the engineering challenges of stellar engineering and the potential benefits for resource extraction

Advanced Robotics: Automating Stellar Mining Operations
- Conceptualization of autonomous robotic systems capable of withstanding extreme stellar conditions
- Exploration of potential mining operations and data-gathering missions near stars
- Discussion on the development of advanced robotic technologies and their applications in space exploration and resource extraction

Chapter 2: Fusion: Unleashing the Power of the Stars

Fusion Basics: A Powerful Energy Source
- Detailed explanation of nuclear fusion and the fusion process
- Discussion on the fusion of atomic nuclei and the energy release mechanism
- Introduction to key concepts such as the fusion fuel cycle, cross-sections, and reaction rates

Confinement Techniques: Containing and Sustaining Fusion Reactions
- In-depth exploration of magnetic confinement methods, including tokamaks and stellarators
- Explanation of the principles behind magnetic fields and their role in confining and controlling the plasma
- Introduction to inertial confinement techniques, such as laser or particle beam-driven fusion, with an emphasis on compression and ignition mechanisms

Ignition and Sustained Fusion: Building a Fusion Reactor
- Step-by-step breakdown of the critical elements required for achieving fusion ignition
- Discussion on the necessary plasma conditions, temperature, and density for successful fusion reactions
- Explanation of the engineering challenges in sustaining a self-sustaining fusion reactor, including heat management and fuel supply

Chapter 3: Nuclea-Thermo and Quantum Thermo Dynamics: The Science of Energy Conversion

Nuclear Thermo Dynamics: Understanding Energy Conversion
- In-depth exploration of nuclear thermodynamics and its applications to energy conversion
- Discussion on energy conservation, entropy, and the laws of thermodynamics as they pertain to nuclear reactions
- Illustration of nuclear thermodynamic concepts using practical examples and calculations

Quantum Thermo Dynamics: Energy at the Quantum Level
- Detailed examination of the intersection between quantum mechanics and thermodynamics
- Explanation of energy quantization, quantum statistical mechanics, and the behavior of energy at the quantum level
- Discussion on the connections between entropy, quantum information, and energy conversion processes

Chapter 4: Global Disarmament and the Pursuit of Peaceful Technologies

Global Disarmament: Promoting Peace and Security
- Detailed exploration of the importance of global disarmament initiatives
- Discussion on the reduction and elimination of nuclear weapons for fostering peace and international security
- Examination of international treaties, arms control agreements, and their impact on disarmament efforts

Promoting Peaceful Technologies: Fusion Energy as a Solution
- In-depth analysis of fusion energy as a sustainable and clean alternative to traditional energy sources
- Discussion on the benefits of fusion technology, including abundant fuel availability, waste minimization, and environmental impact
- Examination of the role of international collaboration, scientific exchange, and diplomacy in advancing peaceful applications of nuclear science

Note: Each chapter can be further expanded with scientific derivations, mathematical equations, case studies, and real-world examples to provide a comprehensive understanding of the topics covered. These additional details would enhance the reader's knowledge of nuclear and quantum thermodynamics, fusion science, and the importance of global disarmament in promoting peaceful technologies.

Chapter 1: Mining Stars: Extracting Resources from the Cosmos

## Mining Stars: Exploring Future Possibilities

In this chapter, we delve into the speculative realm of mining stars and explore potential technologies for extracting resources from these celestial bodies. While current capabilities do not allow us to mine stars, contemplating future possibilities can spark scientific curiosity and innovation.

### Mining Challenges: Extreme Conditions and Vast Distances

Mining stars presents enormous challenges due to their extreme conditions and the vast distances that separate us from them. Stars are immensely hot, composed primarily of hydrogen and helium, and undergo powerful nuclear fusion processes at their cores. The sheer scale and intense energy make it challenging to approach them directly for resource extraction.

### Stellar Engineering: Manipulating Stars for Resource Extraction

One theoretical approach to star mining is through stellar engineering, which involves manipulating a star's energy output or composition to enhance resource availability. This could be achieved through controlled fusion ignition, initiating or modifying specific fusion reactions within a star to generate desired elements or isotopes.

### Advanced Robotics: Automating Stellar Mining Operations

Another avenue to explore is the use of advanced robotics for stellar mining. Autonomous robotic systems designed to withstand the extreme conditions near stars could be deployed for mining operations or data-gathering missions. These robots would need to be capable of withstanding extreme temperatures, intense radiation, and high gravitational forces.

### Resource Extraction Potential: Understanding Star Lifecycles

To identify potential opportunities for resource extraction, it is essential to understand the lifecycles of stars. Exploring the various stages, from star birth to death, can help pinpoint favorable conditions or processes where resources might be more accessible. For example, during supernova explosions, heavy elements can be synthesized and dispersed, potentially providing mining opportunities.

While the concept of mining stars remains highly speculative, considering these theoretical frameworks can inspire future advancements in science and technology. The exploration of stellar engineering and advanced robotics opens up avenues for potential breakthroughs that could revolutionize our understanding of the cosmos and resource utilization.

Note: This chapter provides a brief introduction to the topic of mining stars and serves as a foundation for further exploration in subsequent chapters. To delve deeper into the subject, additional details, scientific theories, and examples would be included in subsequent chapters.

Chapter 2: Fusion: Unleashing the Power of the Stars

Fusion Basics: A Powerful Energy Source

Nuclear fusion is a process that powers stars and holds great promise as a clean and abundant source of energy on Earth. In this chapter, we delve into the fundamental principles of fusion and its potential for practical energy production.

Fusion Reactions: Harnessing the Power of the Nucleus

Fusion reactions involve the fusion of atomic nuclei to form heavier elements, releasing an enormous amount of energy. The most common fusion reaction involves the isotopes of hydrogen: deuterium and tritium. Understanding the fusion fuel cycle, reaction rates, and cross-sections is crucial for achieving controlled fusion.

Plasma State: Creating the Ideal Environment

Fusion reactions occur in a plasma state, where matter is in an ionized gaseous form. The plasma needs to be created and maintained at extremely high temperatures, typically in the range of tens of millions of degrees Celsius, to overcome the Coulomb repulsion between positively charged nuclei.

Confinement Techniques: Controlling the Plasma

To achieve and sustain fusion, effective confinement techniques are necessary. Two prominent methods are magnetic confinement and inertial confinement. Magnetic confinement, utilized in devices like tokamaks and stellarators, uses strong magnetic fields to confine and control the plasma. Inertial confinement relies on compression of a fuel pellet using powerful lasers or particle beams.

Ignition and Sustained Fusion: The Holy Grail of Fusion

Fusion ignition occurs when the energy produced by the fusion reactions is sufficient to sustain the plasma without any external heating. Achieving ignition requires reaching the necessary temperature, density, and confinement time. Research efforts focus on designing systems that can achieve a net energy gain, surpassing the energy input required to sustain the fusion process.

Engineering Challenges: Overcoming Technical Hurdles

Creating a practical fusion reactor poses significant engineering challenges. The extreme conditions, such as the intense heat and radiation, require advanced materials and robust engineering solutions. Furthermore, efficient heat extraction, fuel supply management, and minimizing plasma instabilities are critical factors to address for successful fusion power generation.

The Promise of Fusion Energy: Clean, Safe, and Abundant

Fusion offers numerous advantages as an energy source. It releases energy from abundant fuels, produces no greenhouse gas emissions or long-lived radioactive waste, and offers inherent safety features. The pursuit of fusion as a practical energy solution holds great potential for meeting the world's future energy needs.

Note: This chapter provides a concise overview of fusion, its principles, and the challenges associated with achieving practical fusion power. Subsequent chapters would delve deeper into the technical aspects, research progress, and potential future developments in fusion energy.

Chapter 3: Nuclea-Thermo and Quantum Thermo Dynamics: The Science of Energy Conversion

Nuclear Thermo Dynamics: Understanding Energy Conversion

In this chapter, we delve into the principles of nuclear thermodynamics, which govern the conversion of nuclear energy into usable forms. Understanding these principles is crucial for harnessing the energy released through nuclear reactions.

Energy Conservation: The Law of Conservation of Energy

The law of energy conservation states that energy cannot be created or destroyed but can only be transformed from one form to another. We explore how this fundamental law applies to nuclear reactions and the conversion of nuclear energy into other usable forms, such as thermal or electrical energy.

## Entropy and the Second Law of Thermodynamics: The Direction of Energy Conversion

Entropy, a measure of energy dispersal or disorder, plays a crucial role in energy conversion processes. We delve into the second law of thermodynamics, which states that the entropy of an isolated system tends to increase over time. Understanding entropy enables us to analyze the efficiency and limitations of energy conversion processes, including those involving nuclear reactions.

## Heat Engines and Efficiency: Maximizing Energy Conversion

Heat engines, such as steam turbines or gas turbines, are commonly used to convert thermal energy into mechanical work. We discuss the principles of heat engines, including the Carnot cycle, and explore how efficiency can be maximized by optimizing temperature differentials and minimizing energy losses.

## Nuclear Power Plants: Converting Nuclear Energy into Electricity

Nuclear power plants utilize nuclear reactions to generate heat, which is then converted into electricity. We delve into the working principles of nuclear power plants, including the use of controlled nuclear fission reactions to release heat, which is used to produce steam and drive turbines. We discuss safety measures, waste management, and ongoing advancements in nuclear power plant technology.

## Quantum Thermo Dynamics: Energy at the Quantum Level

In this section, we explore the intersection of quantum mechanics and thermodynamics, known as quantum thermodynamics. Quantum effects become significant at the microscopic scale, where energy quantization and quantum statistical mechanics play a crucial role.

## Energy Quantization: Discrete Energy Levels

Quantum mechanics introduces the concept of discrete energy levels in atoms and subatomic particles. We discuss how energy quantization affects energy conversion processes, including electron transitions and the emission or absorption of photons.

## Statistical Mechanics: Understanding Ensembles and Probability

Statistical mechanics provides a framework for describing the behavior of large systems of particles. We explore the connection between statistical mechanics and thermodynamics, including the Boltzmann distribution, which relates energy and temperature to the probability distribution of particles.

## Quantum Information and Energy Conversion: The Role of Entanglement

Quantum entanglement, the phenomenon where the quantum states of particles are linked, can have implications for energy conversion processes. We discuss how quantum information and entanglement influence energy transfer and efficiency, highlighting the potential for advancements in quantum-enhanced energy conversion technologies.

Note: This chapter provides a concise overview of nuclea-thermo and quantum thermo dynamics, focusing on the fundamental principles of energy conversion. Further chapters would explore more advanced topics, applications, and emerging research areas within these fields.

# Chapter 4: Global Disarmament and the Pursuit of Peaceful Technologies

## Global Disarmament: Promoting Peace and Security

In this chapter, we delve into the importance of global disarmament initiatives and the role they play in fostering peace and international security. We examine the motivations behind disarmament efforts and the benefits they bring to global society.

## The Need for Disarmament: Mitigating the Risks of Nuclear Weapons

We discuss the dangers associated with the proliferation of nuclear weapons, including the potential for catastrophic consequences. We explore the historical context of nuclear arms races and the heightened risks they pose to global stability and peace.

## Arms Control and Non-Proliferation Treaties: Promoting Cooperation

We examine the significance of arms control and non-proliferation treaties in regulating the acquisition, testing, and deployment of nuclear weapons. Examples include the Treaty on the Non-Proliferation of Nuclear Weapons (NPT), the

Comprehensive Nuclear-Test-Ban Treaty (CTBT), and various bilateral agreements between nations.

Multilateral Diplomacy and International Collaboration: Fostering Cooperation

We emphasize the importance of multilateral diplomacy and international collaboration in achieving disarmament goals. We explore the role of international organizations, such as the United Nations and the International Atomic Energy Agency (IAEA), in facilitating dialogue and promoting cooperative disarmament efforts.

Peaceful Uses of Nuclear Science: Redirecting Resources

We discuss how global disarmament initiatives can redirect resources and expertise toward peaceful uses of nuclear science and technology. We examine the potential for repurposing nuclear facilities, knowledge, and capabilities to address pressing global challenges, such as energy security, climate change, and sustainable development.

Fusion Energy and Disarmament: A Shared Goal

We highlight fusion energy as an example of a peaceful technology that aligns with disarmament objectives. Fusion research focuses on harnessing the power of the stars for clean and abundant energy generation, offering an alternative to traditional energy sources that can reduce reliance on fossil fuels and promote environmental sustainability.

Benefits of Disarmament: Enhanced Security and International Cooperation

We discuss the broad benefits that come with global disarmament, including enhanced security, reduced risks of nuclear conflict, and increased trust among nations. Disarmament efforts foster a climate of cooperation and collaboration, allowing for the reallocation of resources towards global challenges and the pursuit of peaceful technologies.

Conclusion: Toward a Peaceful and Secure Future

We conclude the chapter by emphasizing the importance of continued global disarmament efforts. By promoting international cooperation, diplomatic negotiations, and the redirection of resources towards peaceful technologies, we can work toward a more secure and peaceful future for all nations.

Note: This chapter provides a concise overview of the relationship between global disarmament and the pursuit of peaceful technologies. Further chapters would explore specific disarmament treaties, case studies, and ongoing efforts to promote disarmament and peaceful applications of nuclear science.

## Chapter 5: Technological Advancements in Robotic Space Exploration

In this chapter, we delve into the significant advancements in robotic technology that have revolutionized space exploration. We explore the various robotic missions, their capabilities, and the benefits they bring to the field of space exploration.

### Evolution of Robotic Space Exploration: From Early Missions to Current Innovations

We trace the evolution of robotic space exploration, starting from early unmanned missions to the moon and planets. We discuss the groundbreaking achievements of missions such as Voyager, Mars rovers (e.g., Sojourner, Spirit, Opportunity, Curiosity, Perseverance), and the recent successes of robotic landers and orbiters.

### Remote Sensing and Data Collection: Expanding Our Understanding of the Cosmos

We explore how robotic missions enable remote sensing and data collection from distant celestial bodies. Robotic spacecraft equipped with advanced sensors and instruments have provided valuable data on planetary surfaces, atmospheres, and magnetic fields. We discuss the role of robots in collecting high-resolution images, analyzing geological formations, and studying cosmic phenomena.

### Sample Return Missions: Bringing Pieces of the Universe Back to Earth

We examine the significance of sample return missions conducted by robotic spacecraft. These missions, such as the Apollo moon missions and the Hayabusa and OSIRIS-REx missions to asteroids, allow scientists to analyze extraterrestrial samples in terrestrial laboratories, providing critical insights into the origin and composition of celestial bodies.

### Astrobiology and Robotic Missions: Searching for Signs of Life

We delve into the role of robotic missions in the field of astrobiology, where the search for life beyond Earth is a central focus. Robotic explorers, equipped with instruments capable of detecting biomarkers and studying habitability, have expanded our understanding of the potential for life in our solar system and beyond.

Challenges and Future Prospects: Advancing Robotic Space Exploration

We discuss the challenges associated with robotic space exploration, including limited autonomy, communication delays, and the harsh conditions of space environments. We explore ongoing research and development efforts to address these challenges, such as improved robotic autonomy, AI-assisted decision-making, and enhanced mobility capabilities.

Collaboration and the Human-Robot Partnership: Maximizing Mission Success

We emphasize the importance of collaboration between humans and robots in space exploration. Human operators and robotic systems work in tandem, with humans providing high-level decision-making and robots executing complex tasks in hazardous or distant environments. We discuss how this partnership maximizes mission success and allows for a broader range of exploration.

Ethical Considerations and Robotic Space Exploration: Ensuring Responsible Practices

We address ethical considerations related to robotic space exploration, including planetary protection and the preservation of scientifically significant sites. We examine the protocols in place to minimize contamination of celestial bodies and ensure responsible and sustainable exploration practices.

Conclusion: Robotic Space Exploration as the Path to Discoveries

We conclude the chapter by highlighting the crucial role of robotic technology in advancing our knowledge of the cosmos. Robotic missions have revolutionized space exploration, providing invaluable data, expanding our understanding of the universe, and paving the way for future human endeavors in space.

Note: This chapter provides a concise overview of robotic space exploration, focusing on its advancements, capabilities, and future prospects. Subsequent chapters would explore specific missions, technological innovations, and emerging areas within robotic space exploration in greater detail.

## Chapter 6: Space Mining and Resource Utilization

In this chapter, we delve into the emerging field of space mining and resource utilization. We explore the potential for extracting valuable resources from celestial bodies, the technologies involved, and the implications for future space exploration and human activities beyond Earth.

### The Promise of Space Mining: Expanding Resource Accessibility

We discuss the motivation behind space mining, which is to access and utilize the vast resources present in space. The availability of resources such as water, metals, and minerals on celestial bodies like the Moon, asteroids, and Mars holds the potential to enable sustainable human activities in space and support future deep space missions.

### Resource Prospecting and Characterization: Identifying Valuable Deposits

We examine the techniques and instruments used in resource prospecting and characterization. Remote sensing technologies, robotic missions, and in situ analysis play crucial roles in identifying and evaluating potential resource deposits. We discuss how data collected from these missions informs future mining operations.

### In-Situ Resource Utilisation: Making Space Self-Sufficient

We explore the concept of in-situ resource utilisation (ISRU), which involves extracting and processing resources on-site for immediate use in space missions. ISRU aims to reduce the dependence on Earth for supplies and fuel, making space exploration more self-sufficient and sustainable. We discuss potential ISRU techniques, such as extracting water ice for life support systems or producing rocket propellant.

### Mining Technologies and Techniques: Extracting Resources in Space

We delve into the technologies and techniques required for space mining. Concepts such as excavation, drilling, and resource extraction in low-gravity or vacuum environments pose unique challenges. We explore robotic systems, autonomous mining equipment, and innovative approaches for resource extraction and processing.

### Resource Processing and Refining: Turning Raw Materials into Usable Products

We discuss the importance of resource processing and refining in space mining operations. Raw materials extracted from celestial bodies often require further processing to convert them into usable products. We examine technologies for refining ores, separating desired elements, and manufacturing products for various space applications.

Infrastructure and Logistics: Supporting Space Mining Operations

Space mining operations require infrastructure and logistical support. We explore the concept of a lunar or asteroid base, where mining activities can be conducted and resources can be processed. We discuss the challenges of establishing and maintaining such infrastructure, including power generation, waste management, and transportation systems.

Legal and Policy Considerations: Governance of Space Resources

We examine the legal and policy frameworks surrounding space mining and resource utilization. The international community is working to establish guidelines and regulations to ensure responsible and equitable resource extraction practices. We discuss ongoing discussions, treaties, and the importance of international collaboration in addressing the governance of space resources.

Implications for Future Space Exploration: Enabling Human Expansion

We explore the implications of space mining and resource utilization for future space exploration and human expansion beyond Earth. Access to local resources reduces the cost and logistical challenges of space missions, enabling sustained human presence on celestial bodies and facilitating long-duration missions to deep space destinations.

Conclusion: The Dawn of Space Resource Utilization

We conclude the chapter by highlighting the significance of space mining and resource utilization in unlocking the potential of space exploration. As technology advances and our understanding of celestial bodies expands, the extraction and utilization of space resources will play a vital role in shaping the future of human activities in space.

Note: This chapter provides a concise overview of space mining and resource utilization. Further chapters could explore specific resource extraction methods, case studies of robotic mining missions, policy developments, and ongoing research in greater detail.

Chapter 7: The Future of Interstellar Travel: Exploring Beyond our Solar System

In this chapter, we embark on an exploration of the future of interstellar travel, discussing the challenges, theoretical possibilities, and potential technological advancements that could one day allow us to venture beyond our solar system.

Interstellar Travel: A Grand Human Endeavor

We introduce the concept of interstellar travel, which involves journeying to other star systems outside our own. We discuss the motivations for interstellar exploration, including the quest for scientific knowledge, the search for extraterrestrial life, and the expansion of human civilization.

The Challenges of Interstellar Travel: Overcoming Cosmic Hurdles

We delve into the immense challenges associated with interstellar travel, including the vast distances between star systems, the need for propulsion systems capable of reaching relativistic speeds, and the preservation of human life during long-duration space journeys. We explore potential solutions to these challenges and the technological advancements required.

Propulsion Systems: Pushing the Boundaries of Speed

We examine various theoretical propulsion systems that could enable interstellar travel. Concepts such as nuclear propulsion, antimatter propulsion, and exotic technologies like warp drives and wormholes are discussed, highlighting the scientific principles behind them and their potential feasibility.

Relativistic Effects and Time Dilation: The Impact on Human Experience

We explore the consequences of traveling at relativistic speeds, where time dilation and other relativistic effects become significant. We discuss how these effects would impact the experience of space travelers, including the passage of time, aging, and communication with Earth.

Generation Ships and Sleeper Ships: Sustaining Long-Duration Journeys

We examine the concept of generation ships, where multiple generations of humans would be born and live onboard a spacecraft during an interstellar journey. We discuss the challenges of maintaining a self-sustaining ecosystem and the social implications of such long-duration voyages. Additionally, we explore the possibility of sleeper ships, where humans enter a state of suspended animation for the duration of the journey.

Exploring Exoplanets: Targeting Habitable Worlds

We discuss the exciting prospect of exploring exoplanets, planets orbiting stars outside our solar system. We explore methods for detecting exoplanets, including transit photometry and radial velocity measurements, and highlight the importance of identifying potentially habitable worlds for future interstellar missions.

Interstellar Communication: Bridging the Cosmic Divide

We delve into the challenges of interstellar communication, given the vast distances and signal delays involved. We explore methods for long-distance communication, such as laser-based communication systems and interstellar messaging strategies.

Ethical Considerations: Preserving the Integrity of Interstellar Exploration

We address ethical considerations related to interstellar travel, including the potential impact on extraterrestrial life, the responsible use of resources, and the preservation of celestial environments. We discuss the importance of responsible exploration and the establishment of ethical guidelines to guide our interstellar endeavors.

Conclusion: The Human Spirit of Exploration

We conclude the chapter by emphasizing the indomitable human spirit of exploration and the boundless curiosity that drives us to venture into the unknown. While interstellar travel poses tremendous challenges, scientific and technological advancements, along with a collaborative global effort, may one day make interstellar exploration a reality.

Note: This chapter provides a concise overview of the future of interstellar travel. Further chapters could delve into specific propulsion technologies, mission concepts, potential target star systems, and ongoing research in the field of interstellar travel.

As of now, there are no specific established guidelines for interstellar travel, as it remains a hypothetical and highly challenging endeavor. However, ethical considerations and responsible exploration can serve as guiding principles for future interstellar travel. Here are some suggested guidelines to consider:

1. Environmental Preservation: Ensure the preservation and minimal disruption of celestial environments and ecosystems encountered during interstellar travel. Minimize the contamination of potentially habitable planets or moons with Earth-based microbes to preserve their scientific integrity and potential for life.

2. Scientific Collaboration: Foster international scientific collaboration to share knowledge, resources, and expertise in interstellar travel. Collaboration promotes the responsible and efficient advancement of technology, safety standards, and exploration protocols.

3. Respect for Extraterrestrial Life: Prioritize the search for and protection of potential extraterrestrial life. Establish protocols to avoid contamination and interference with indigenous life forms, respecting their potential significance and promoting scientific understanding.

4. Sustainable Resource Utilization: Develop sustainable practices for resource utilization during interstellar travel. Minimize waste, maximize recycling, and explore in-situ resource utilization to reduce the reliance on Earth-based supplies and minimize the ecological impact of space exploration.

5. Safety and Well-being of Space Travelers: Ensure the safety, health, and well-being of space travelers during interstellar journeys. Mitigate the physical and psychological challenges of long-duration space travel, provide adequate life support systems, and establish protocols for medical emergencies and psychological support.

6. Long-Term Planning and Self-Sufficiency: Plan for self-sufficiency and sustainability during interstellar missions. Consider the establishment of self-sustaining ecosystems, generation ships, or other means to ensure the long-term viability of human populations during lengthy journeys.

7. Openness and Transparency: Promote openness and transparency in interstellar exploration. Share findings, data, and discoveries with the global scientific community and the public, fostering a sense of inclusivity and promoting a better understanding of the universe.

8. Respect for Cultural and Historical Significance: Show respect for cultural and historical artifacts encountered during interstellar exploration. Establish protocols for their preservation and study, ensuring that they are treated with sensitivity and respect.

9. Compliance with International Laws and Treaties: Abide by international laws, regulations, and treaties governing space exploration and activities. Respect existing agreements related to celestial bodies, such as the Outer Space Treaty, and support efforts to develop new legal frameworks specific to interstellar travel.

These guidelines are meant to provide a starting point for discussions and considerations regarding the ethical and responsible aspects of interstellar travel. As the field progresses and the potential for interstellar missions becomes more tangible, it is essential to continue engaging in ethical debates and establish specific guidelines that address the unique challenges and complexities of interstellar exploration.

Creating a hologram involves a combination of optical physics, projection techniques, and display technologies. While I can't physically assist you in inventing a hologram, I can provide you with a basic understanding of how holograms work and some steps you can take to create a simple holographic projection.

1. Understanding holography:
Holography is a technique that allows the recording and reconstruction of three-dimensional images. It utilizes the interference patterns between laser light beams to capture and display images with depth and realism.

2. Basic holographic setup:
To create a simple hologram, you would need the following components:
- Laser: A coherent light source, typically a laser, to produce a stable and monochromatic light beam.
- Beam splitter: A device that splits the laser beam into two separate beams.
- Object beam: One of the split beams that illuminates the object you want to record as a hologram.
- Reference beam: The other split beam that serves as a reference for interference.
- Holographic film: A medium that records the interference pattern formed by the object and reference beams.

- Reconstruction beam: A laser beam that illuminates the developed holographic film to reconstruct the recorded image.

3. Hologram creation process:
Here is a simplified overview of the hologram creation process:
- Set up a darkened room and position the holographic film.
- Split the laser beam into object and reference beams using a beam splitter.
- Illuminate the object with the object beam, allowing the reflected or scattered light to interfere with the reference beam.
- Capture the interference pattern on the holographic film, which records the phase and amplitude information of the object's light.
- Develop the holographic film.
- Illuminate the developed film with the reconstruction beam, reconstructing the recorded object as a three-dimensional image.

4. Limitations and advancements:
Creating true, full-color holograms with dynamic objects is still a complex and challenging task. However, advancements in technology, such as spatial light modulators, computer-generated holography, and digital holography, have allowed for more advanced holographic displays and interactive experiences.

Remember, inventing a hologram involves a deep understanding of optics, lasers, and materials. It requires expertise in physics and engineering, as well as access to specialized equipment. If you're serious about inventing a hologram, I recommend studying these fields or collaborating with experts in the field of holography.

Title: "Exploring Holography: Unveiling the Art and Science of Three-Dimensional Imaging"

Introduction:
Welcome to "Exploring Holography," a comprehensive guide that delves into the captivating world of holographic imaging. In this book, we will embark on a journey to understand the principles, techniques, and potential applications of holography. Whether you're a curious enthusiast, a student of physics, or a budding holography inventor, this book will serve as a valuable resource on your path to mastering the art of creating holograms.

Chapter 1: The Foundation of Holography
- An overview of the history and evolution of holography.
- The fundamental concepts of interference, diffraction, and wavefront reconstruction.

- Introduction to holographic film and its role in capturing interference patterns.

Chapter 2: Light and Lasers
- The properties of light and the importance of coherence for holography.
- Laser technology and its application in holography.
- Types of lasers commonly used for hologram creation.

Chapter 3: Building Your Holographic Set-Up
- A detailed guide to constructing a basic holographic set-up.
- Selection and alignment of optical components, including beam splitters and mirrors.
- Considerations for creating a controlled and stable environment.

Chapter 4: Hologram Recording Techniques
- Understanding object and reference beams and their interaction.
- Techniques for illuminating the object and capturing interference patterns.
- Types of holographic film and their characteristics.

Chapter 5: Developing and Processing Holographic Film
- Chemical processes involved in developing holographic film.
- Techniques for processing holographic film to reveal the recorded interference patterns.
- Safety precautions and handling guidelines for working with holographic film.

Chapter 6: Reconstruction and Displaying Holograms
- Reconstruction beam generation and its role in reviving the recorded holographic image.
- Types of reconstruction methods and their respective advantages.
- Display technologies for visualizing and experiencing holograms.

Chapter 7: Advanced Holography Techniques
- Computer-generated holography (CGH) and digital holography.
- Techniques for creating full-color holograms.
- Advancements in holographic displays and interactive experiences.

Chapter 8: Practical Applications of Holography
- Current and potential applications of holography in various fields.
- Holography as an art form and its impact on visual expression.
- Innovations and future possibilities in holographic technology.

Conclusion:
As we conclude our journey through the fascinating realm of holography, we hope this book has provided you with a solid foundation in understanding and creating holograms. Remember, holography is an interdisciplinary field that combines art, science, and engineering. With dedication, practice, and a thirst for knowledge, you can continue pushing the boundaries of holographic imaging and contribute to the ever-evolving world of three-dimensional visualization.

Appendix:
- Glossary of key terms and concepts.
- Additional resources for further exploration.
- Troubleshooting common issues encountered in hologram creation.

Note: While this book provides a comprehensive overview of holography, it's important to note that actually inventing a hologram may require more extensive study, hands-on experience, and collaboration with experts in the field.

Title: "Exploring Holography: Unveiling the Art and Science of Three-Dimensional Imaging"

Introduction:
Welcome to "Exploring Holography," a comprehensive guide that delves into the captivating world of holographic imaging. In this book, we will embark on a journey to understand the principles, techniques, and potential applications of holography. Whether you're a curious enthusiast, a student of physics, or a budding holography inventor, this book will serve as a valuable resource on your path to mastering the art of creating holograms.

Chapter 1: The Foundation of Holography
- An overview of the history and evolution of holography.
- The fundamental concepts of interference, diffraction, and wavefront reconstruction.
- Introduction to holographic film and its role in capturing interference patterns.

Chapter 2: Light and Lasers
- The properties of light and the importance of coherence for holography.
- Laser technology and its application in holography.
- Types of lasers commonly used for hologram creation.

Chapter 3: Building Your Holographic Set-Up

- A detailed guide to constructing a basic holographic set-up.
- Selection and alignment of optical components, including beam splitters and mirrors.
- Considerations for creating a controlled and stable environment.

Chapter 4: Hologram Recording Techniques
- Understanding object and reference beams and their interaction.
- Techniques for illuminating the object and capturing interference patterns.
- Types of holographic film and their characteristics.

Chapter 5: Developing and Processing Holographic Film
- Chemical processes involved in developing holographic film.
- Techniques for processing holographic film to reveal the recorded interference patterns.
- Safety precautions and handling guidelines for working with holographic film.

Chapter 6: Reconstruction and Displaying Holograms
- Reconstruction beam generation and its role in reviving the recorded holographic image.
- Types of reconstruction methods and their respective advantages.
- Display technologies for visualizing and experiencing holograms.

Chapter 7: Advanced Holography Techniques
- Computer-generated holography (CGH) and digital holography.
- Techniques for creating full-color holograms.
- Advancements in holographic displays and interactive experiences.

Chapter 8: Practical Applications of Holography
- Current and potential applications of holography in various fields.
- Holography as an art form and its impact on visual expression.
- Innovations and future possibilities in holographic technology.

Conclusion:
As we conclude our journey through the fascinating realm of holography, we hope this book has provided you with a solid foundation in understanding and creating holograms. Remember, holography is an interdisciplinary field that combines art, science, and engineering. With dedication, practice, and a thirst for knowledge, you can continue pushing the boundaries of holographic imaging and contribute to the ever-evolving world of three-dimensional visualization.

Appendix:
- Glossary of key terms and concepts.
- Additional resources for further exploration.
- Troubleshooting common issues encountered in hologram creation.

Note: While this book provides a comprehensive overview of holography, it's important to note that actually inventing a hologram may require more extensive study, hands-on experience, and collaboration with experts in the field.

Chapter 2: Light and Lasers

Introduction:
In Chapter 2, we will delve into the properties of light and explore the role of lasers in holography. Understanding the characteristics of light and utilizing coherent light sources are essential for successful hologram creation.

2.1 The Nature of Light
- The electromagnetic spectrum: A broad range of light wavelengths.
- Photons: The particles of light and their behavior.
- Properties of light: Reflection, refraction, absorption, and transmission.

2.2 Coherence and Laser Light
- Coherence in light: The importance of consistent phase relationship between light waves.
- Incoherent light vs. coherent light: Understanding the distinction.
- Laser light: Characteristics that make lasers ideal for holography.

2.3 Laser Technology
- Laser components: Gain medium, pump source, and optical cavity.
- Types of lasers: Gas lasers, solid-state lasers, and diode lasers.
- Laser parameters: Wavelength, power, and stability.

2.4 Laser Safety
- Laser hazards: Understanding the potential risks associated with laser use.
- Laser safety measures: Protective eyewear, controlled environments, and safety protocols.
- Compliance with laser safety standards and regulations.

2.5 Laser Applications in Holography
- Laser as a light source for holography: Its role in providing coherent light.
- Spatial coherence: Ensuring consistent wavefronts for interference.
- Techniques for laser beam shaping and manipulation.

2.6 Non-laser Light Sources
- Alternative light sources for holography: LEDs, white light sources, and more.
- Trade-offs and considerations when using non-laser light sources.
- Advancements in non-laser holographic techniques.

Conclusion:
In this chapter, we have explored the properties of light, the concept of coherence, and the role of lasers in holography. Understanding the nature of light and harnessing the power of lasers are crucial for capturing high-quality interference patterns and achieving successful holographic imaging. In the next chapter, we will focus on building a holographic set-up, selecting appropriate components, and ensuring a controlled environment for hologram creation.

Chapter 3: Building Your Holographic Set-Up

Introduction:
In the previous chapter, we delved into the properties of light and the role of lasers in holography. Now, we will take the next step and explore the construction of a holographic set-up. Building a well-designed and stable set-up is crucial for capturing high-quality holograms. In this chapter, we will discuss the essential components, their functions, and considerations for creating an effective holographic system.

3.1 Darkened Room and Optical Table
- Importance of a darkened room: Minimizing external light interference.
- Creating a controlled environment: Light-proofing, vibration isolation, and temperature control.
- Optical table: Its role in providing stability and a vibration-free platform for optical components.

3.2 Laser System
- Selecting the appropriate laser: Considerations for power, wavelength, and coherence.
- Laser mounting and alignment: Ensuring proper stability and alignment of the laser beam.
- Laser safety measures: Implementing safety interlocks, emergency stop buttons, and laser enclosures.

3.3 Beam Splitter and Optics

- Beam splitter: Choosing the right type and quality for dividing the laser beam.
- Mirrors and lenses: Manipulating the laser beam for proper beam shaping and alignment.
- Optics mounting and alignment: Securing and aligning optical components for optimal performance.

3.4 Object Table and Stage
- Object table: Providing a stable surface for placing the object to be recorded.
- Stage and positioning system: Facilitating controlled movement and precise positioning of the object.
- Considerations for minimizing vibrations and ensuring stability during object illumination.

3.5 Holographic Film or Recording Medium
- Selection of holographic film: Understanding characteristics such as sensitivity, resolution, and processing requirements.
- Handling and loading holographic film: Techniques for preventing damage and contamination.
- Film holders and frames: Securing the holographic film during exposure and development processes.

3.6 Environmental Control
- Temperature and humidity control: Maintaining optimal conditions for hologram recording and film processing.
- Ventilation and air filtration: Reducing contaminants that can affect hologram quality.
- Light shielding and stray light control: Preventing unwanted light from interfering with hologram recording.

3.7 Laboratory Safety
- Laser safety precautions: Laser goggles, safety protocols, and adherence to regulations.
- Chemical safety: Handling and storage of chemicals used in film development processes.
- Emergency preparedness: Safety equipment, emergency procedures, and first aid.

Conclusion:
In this chapter, we explored the essential components and considerations for constructing a holographic set-up. From creating a controlled environment to selecting the appropriate laser system, beam splitters, optics, and positioning

systems, each element plays a crucial role in capturing high-quality holograms. Additionally, we discussed environmental control and laboratory safety to ensure a safe and optimized working environment. With a well-designed set-up, we are now ready to move forward and delve into the hologram recording techniques in the next chapter.

## Chapter 4: Hologram Recording Techniques

Introduction:
Having constructed a well-designed holographic set-up, we are now ready to explore the techniques used to record holograms. In this chapter, we will delve into the process of illuminating the object, capturing the interference patterns, and recording them on the holographic film or other recording mediums. Understanding these techniques is vital for achieving accurate and high-quality hologram recordings.

### 4.1 Illumination Techniques
- Direct illumination: Placing the object directly in the path of the object beam.
- Relay optics: Using lenses or mirrors to redirect and focus the object beam onto the object.
- Off-axis illumination: Angling the object beam to minimize unwanted reflections or diffraction effects.

### 4.2 Object Preparation and Handling
- Object selection: Choosing objects suitable for holographic recording.
- Object positioning and stability: Ensuring the object remains steady during the recording process.
- Handling precautions: Minimizing physical contact, vibrations, and unwanted reflections.

### 4.3 Reference Beam Configuration
- Generating the reference beam: Proper alignment and stability of the reference beam.
- Reference beam size and shape: Controlling the reference beam parameters for optimal interference.

### 4.4 Interference Pattern Formation
- Interference fringes: How the object and reference beams interfere to create the pattern.
- Recording distance: Determining the distance between the object and the holographic film.

- Adjusting exposure time: Achieving the right balance between overexposure and underexposure.

4.5 Holographic Film and Exposure Techniques
- Loading the holographic film: Ensuring proper alignment and avoiding contamination.
- Exposure control: Controlling the intensity and duration of the exposure.
- Multiple exposures and multiplexing: Recording multiple holograms on a single film.

4.6 Film Development and Processing
- Developing the holographic film: Chemical processes to reveal the recorded interference patterns.
- Stop bath and fixing: Halting development and removing unexposed or undeveloped silver halide crystals.
- Washing and drying: Rinsing the film to remove residual chemicals and ensuring proper drying.

4.7 Digital Holography Techniques
- Introduction to digital holography: Recording holograms using digital sensors and processing techniques.
- Advantages and limitations of digital holography: Real-time visualization, computational capabilities, and storage.

Conclusion:
In this chapter, we explored the techniques involved in recording holograms. From illumination techniques to object preparation, reference beam configuration, interference pattern formation, and film development, each step is critical for capturing accurate and high-quality holograms. Additionally, we touched upon digital holography as an emerging technique that leverages digital sensors and computational methods. With a solid understanding of hologram recording techniques, we are now equipped to move forward and explore the reconstruction and display of holograms in the upcoming chapters.

Chapter 5: Reconstruction and Displaying Holograms

Introduction:
With the hologram recorded on the film or captured digitally, the next step is to reconstruct the recorded interference pattern and bring the holographic image to life. In this chapter, we will explore the techniques and technologies used for reconstructing and displaying holograms, allowing us to experience the three-dimensional nature of the recorded objects.

5.1 Reconstruction Methods
- Optical reconstruction: Illuminating the holographic film with a reconstruction beam.
- Denisyuk and Leith-Upatnieks setups: Classic optical reconstruction configurations.
- Digital reconstruction: Using computational algorithms to reconstruct digital holograms.

5.2 Collimated and Divergent Reconstruction
- Collimated reconstruction: Producing a collimated or parallel beam for visualizing the hologram.
- Divergent reconstruction: Creating a divergent beam to reconstruct the hologram at a specific viewing distance.

5.3 Real and Virtual Images
- Real image reconstruction: Forming a physical image that can be observed without additional aids.
- Virtual image reconstruction: Producing an image that appears to be floating in space.

5.4 Display Technologies for Holograms
- Transmission displays: Using transparent screens to project holographic images.
- Reflection displays: Employing reflective surfaces for hologram visualization.
- Spatial light modulators: Dynamic holographic displays with electronically controlled pixels.

5.5 Holographic Optical Elements
- Introduction to holographic optical elements (HOEs): Recording optical components in holographic form.
- Applications of HOEs: Diffraction gratings, beam splitters, lenses, and more.
- Design considerations and fabrication techniques for HOEs.

5.6 Holographic Projection and Projection Surfaces
- Projection systems for large-scale holograms: Challenges and solutions.
- Projection surfaces and diffusers: Enhancing holographic image quality and visibility.
- Optimization of viewing conditions: Lighting and background considerations for an optimal hologram viewing experience.

5.7 Interactive Holography
- Touchable holograms: Haptic feedback and interaction with holographic objects.
- Augmented reality (AR) and mixed reality (MR) holography: Merging holograms with the real-world environment.

Conclusion:
In this chapter, we explored the techniques and technologies used for reconstructing and displaying holograms. From optical reconstruction methods to digital reconstruction algorithms, collimated and divergent reconstruction, and various display technologies, each approach offers unique advantages and challenges. We also touched upon the exciting developments in interactive holography, allowing users to physically interact with holographic objects. With a solid understanding of hologram reconstruction and display, we can now fully appreciate the three-dimensional beauty of holographic imaging.

Chapter 5: Reconstruction and Displaying Holograms

Introduction:
With the hologram recorded on the film or captured digitally, the next step is to reconstruct the recorded interference pattern and bring the holographic image to life. In this chapter, we will explore the techniques and technologies used for reconstructing and displaying holograms, allowing us to experience the three-dimensional nature of the recorded objects.

5.1 Reconstruction Methods
- Optical reconstruction: Illuminating the holographic film with a reconstruction beam.
- Denisyuk and Leith-Upatnieks setups: Classic optical reconstruction configurations.
- Digital reconstruction: Using computational algorithms to reconstruct digital holograms.

5.2 Collimated and Divergent Reconstruction
- Collimated reconstruction: Producing a collimated or parallel beam for visualizing the hologram.
- Divergent reconstruction: Creating a divergent beam to reconstruct the hologram at a specific viewing distance.

5.3 Real and Virtual Images
- Real image reconstruction: Forming a physical image that can be observed without additional aids.

- Virtual image reconstruction: Producing an image that appears to be floating in space.

5.4 Display Technologies for Holograms

- Transmission displays: Using transparent screens to project holographic images.
- Reflection displays: Employing reflective surfaces for hologram visualization.
- Spatial light modulators: Dynamic holographic displays with electronically controlled pixels.

5.5 Holographic Optical Elements

- Introduction to holographic optical elements (HOEs): Recording optical components in holographic form.
- Applications of HOEs: Diffraction gratings, beam splitters, lenses, and more.
- Design considerations and fabrication techniques for HOEs.

5.6 Holographic Projection and Projection Surfaces

- Projection systems for large-scale holograms: Challenges and solutions.
- Projection surfaces and diffusers: Enhancing holographic image quality and visibility.
- Optimization of viewing conditions: Lighting and background considerations for an optimal hologram viewing experience.

5.7 Interactive Holography

- Touchable holograms: Haptic feedback and interaction with holographic objects.
- Augmented reality (AR) and mixed reality (MR) holography: Merging holograms with the real-world environment.

Conclusion:

In this chapter, we explored the techniques and technologies used for reconstructing and displaying holograms. From optical reconstruction methods to digital reconstruction algorithms, collimated and divergent reconstruction, and various display technologies, each approach offers unique advantages and challenges. We also touched upon the exciting developments in interactive holography, allowing users to physically interact with holographic objects. With a solid understanding of hologram reconstruction and display, we can now fully appreciate the three-dimensional beauty of holographic imaging.

Chapter 6: Advanced Holography Techniques

Introduction:
In the previous chapters, we explored the foundational aspects of holography, including recording techniques and hologram reconstruction. In this chapter, we will delve into advanced holography techniques that push the boundaries of traditional holography. From computer-generated holography (CGH) to full-color holography and emerging technologies, we will explore the cutting-edge developments that are shaping the future of holographic imaging.

6.1 Computer-Generated Holography (CGH)
- Introduction to CGH: Creating holograms computationally using algorithms.
- CGH workflow: From 3D object modeling to hologram computation.
- Advantages and applications of CGH: Realistic 3D imaging, data storage, and security.

6.2 Digital Holography
- Principles of digital holography: Recording holograms using digital sensors and numerical reconstruction.
- Techniques for digital hologram acquisition: In-line holography, off-axis holography, and phase-shifting holography.
- Digital hologram processing and reconstruction: Computational algorithms for visualization.

6.3 Full-Color Holography
- Challenges in achieving full-color holography: Overcoming limitations of spectral recording and reconstruction.
- Techniques for full-color holography: RGB color separation, multi-layer holography, and spatial light modulators.
- Applications of full-color holography: 3D visualization, art, and entertainment.

6.4 Holographic Printing
- Introduction to holographic printing: Creating physical holograms in a printable format.
- Techniques for holographic printing: Embossing, lithography, and laser-induced printing.
- Applications of holographic printing: Security features, packaging, and artistic expression.

6.5 Holographic Optical Tweezers
- Principles of holographic optical tweezers: Manipulating microscopic objects using holographic traps.

- Techniques for holographic optical tweezers: Generating complex trapping patterns and controlling multiple traps.
- Applications of holographic optical tweezers: Biological research, microfabrication, and nanotechnology.

6.6 Plenoptic Holography
- Introduction to plenoptic holography: Capturing both spatial and angular information of a scene.
- Techniques for plenoptic holography: Array of micro-lenses, light-field imaging, and computational reconstruction.
- Applications of plenoptic holography: 3D displays, virtual reality, and imaging systems.

6.7 Emerging Holographic Technologies
- Advancements in holographic displays: Light field displays, holographic waveguides, and volumetric displays.
- Nanotechnology and holography: Manipulating light at the nanoscale for advanced holographic applications.
- Quantum holography: Exploring the intersection of quantum mechanics and holography.

Conclusion:
In this chapter, we explored advanced holography techniques that are at the forefront of holographic imaging. From computer-generated holography and full-color holography to holographic printing, optical tweezers, plenoptic holography, and emerging technologies, these advancements are shaping the future of holography. As technology continues to evolve, the possibilities for holographic imaging are expanding, opening up new avenues for scientific research, entertainment, art, and many other fields. With a glimpse into these advanced techniques, we can now envision the exciting potential that lies ahead in the world of holography.

Chapter 7: Practical Applications of Holography

Introduction:
Holography, with its ability to capture and display three-dimensional images, holds immense potential across various fields. In this chapter, we will explore the practical applications of holography, showcasing how this fascinating technology is making an impact in diverse industries. From medicine and engineering to art and entertainment, holography is revolutionizing the way we visualize and interact with the world around us.

7.1 Medical Imaging and Visualization
- Holographic imaging in medical diagnostics: Advancements in holographic microscopy and tomography.
- Surgical guidance and training: Holographic displays for real-time visualizations during surgeries.
- Holography in medical education: Simulating anatomical structures and medical scenarios.

7.2 Engineering and Design
- Holography in product design and prototyping: Creating three-dimensional virtual models.
- Industrial inspection and quality control: Using holographic imaging for precise measurements and defect detection.
- Engineering simulations and virtual prototyping: Enhancing design processes with interactive holographic displays.

7.3 Data Visualization and Analytics
- Holographic data visualization: Conveying complex data in an intuitive and immersive manner.
- Augmented reality (AR) and holographic interfaces: Visualizing digital information in the real world.
- Holography in scientific research: Analyzing and presenting research data in three-dimensional formats.

7.4 Art, Entertainment, and Advertising
- Holographic art installations: Creating interactive and visually stunning holographic artworks.
- Holographic stage performances and concerts: Enhancing live performances with holographic projections.
- Holographic advertising and marketing: Engaging consumers with captivating holographic displays.

7.5 Security and Authentication
- Holographic security features: Using holograms for anti-counterfeiting measures on identification cards, banknotes, and products.
- Holographic authentication and encryption: Leveraging holography for secure data transmission and identification.

7.6 Education and Training
- Holography in education: Enhancing science, technology, engineering, and mathematics (STEM) education with interactive holograms.

- Virtual reality (VR) and holographic simulations: Creating immersive training environments for various industries.

7.7 Astronomical and Aerospace Applications
- Holography in astronomy: Visualizing celestial bodies and structures in three dimensions.
- Holography in aerospace engineering: Simulating spacecraft designs and analyzing aerodynamic properties.

Conclusion:
In this chapter, we explored the practical applications of holography across various industries. From medical imaging and engineering to data visualization, art, entertainment, security, education, and aerospace, holography is transforming the way we perceive and interact with the world. As holographic technologies continue to advance, we can expect to see even more innovative applications and groundbreaking developments in the future. Holography is an exciting and ever-evolving field that holds immense promise for the advancement of science, technology, and human creativity.

## Chapter 8: Innovations and Future Possibilities in Holography

Introduction:
In this final chapter, we will explore the innovations and future possibilities in the field of holography. Holography has come a long way since its inception, and advancements continue to push the boundaries of what is possible. From advancements in display technologies to emerging applications and groundbreaking research, holography is poised to revolutionize various industries and open up new avenues of exploration.

8.1 Advancements in Holographic Displays
- High-resolution holographic displays: Achieving greater image quality and clarity.
- Scalable holographic displays: Enabling larger and more immersive holographic experiences.
- Lightweight and portable holographic displays: Expanding the accessibility and usability of holography.

8.2 Holography and Artificial Intelligence (AI)
- AI-assisted holographic imaging: Improving hologram generation, reconstruction, and processing.
- Holographic AI assistants: Integrating holograms with AI-powered virtual assistants for enhanced user interaction.

8.3 Holography and Internet of Things (IoT)
- Holographic interfaces for IoT devices: Visualizing and interacting with IoT data in a three-dimensional space.
- Holographic telepresence and remote collaboration: Enabling realistic and immersive communication experiences.

8.4 Holography and Quantum Technologies
- Quantum holography: Leveraging quantum principles for secure holographic imaging and communication.
- Quantum computing and holographic simulations: Exploiting quantum systems for faster and more efficient holographic calculations.

8.5 Biomedical Applications of Holography
- Holographic tissue engineering and regenerative medicine: Creating three-dimensional structures for organ replacement.
- Holographic microscopy for cellular imaging: Advancing diagnostic capabilities and cellular research.

8.6 Holography and Energy Efficiency
- Energy-efficient holographic displays: Developing holographic technologies that minimize power consumption.
- Holographic solar energy concentration: Utilizing holograms for efficient solar energy capture and conversion.

8.7 Holography in Virtual and Mixed Reality
- Holographic virtual reality (VR) experiences: Blending holograms with virtual environments for enhanced immersion.
- Mixed reality (MR) holography: Combining holograms with the real world to create interactive and engaging experiences.

Conclusion:
In this final chapter, we explored the innovations and future possibilities in the field of holography. From advancements in holographic displays and the integration of AI and IoT to the intersection of holography with quantum technologies, biomedical applications, energy efficiency, and virtual/mixed reality, holography is poised to reshape various industries and revolutionize human experiences. The future of holography holds tremendous promise, and as researchers, engineers, and creators continue to push the boundaries of this technology, we can anticipate even more remarkable advancements and applications in the years to come. Holography has the potential to transform the way we per-

ceive and interact with the world, opening up new frontiers of exploration and expanding our understanding of reality itself.

Appendix:

Glossary of Key Terms and Concepts

- Holography: The technique of recording and reconstructing three-dimensional images using interference patterns.
- Coherence: The property of light waves where they have a consistent phase relationship.
- Interference: The phenomenon that occurs when two or more light waves combine, resulting in constructive or destructive interference patterns.
- Diffraction: The bending or spreading of light waves as they pass through an aperture or encounter an obstacle.
- Wavefront: A surface representing points of equal phase in a propagating wave.
- Laser: An acronym for Light Amplification by Stimulated Emission of Radiation, it is a device that emits coherent light through the process of stimulated emission.
- Beam splitter: An optical device that splits a beam of light into two or more separate beams.
- Holographic film: A photosensitive material that records the interference pattern between an object beam and a reference beam.
- Reconstruction beam: The coherent light beam used to illuminate the holographic film and reconstruct the recorded image.
- Transmission hologram: A hologram that becomes visible when light is transmitted through it.
- Reflection hologram: A hologram that becomes visible when light is reflected off its surface.
- Computer-generated holography (CGH): The creation of holograms using computational algorithms and digital models of objects.
- Full-color holography: The recording and display of holograms that accurately reproduce the colors of the original scene.
- Holographic optical elements (HOEs): Holograms that perform specific optical functions, such as diffraction, beam splitting, and focusing.
- Plenoptic holography: A technique that captures both spatial and angular information of a scene, allowing for post-capture refocusing and viewpoint changes.
- Holographic printing: The process of creating physical holograms using printing techniques, such as embossing or laser-induced printing.

- Holographic optical tweezers: A technique that uses holography to manipulate microscopic objects by creating optical traps.
- Quantum holography: The exploration of the relationship between holography and quantum information theory, aiming to develop holographic principles within a quantum framework.

Additional Resources for Further Exploration

- Books:
  1. "Principles of Holography" by Howard M. Smith
  2. "Holography: A Practical Approach" by Gerhard K. Ackermann
  3. "Holography Handbook" by Fred Unterseher, Bob Schlesinger, and Jean-Marc Paviot

- Journals and Research Papers:
  1. Optics Express
  2. Journal of Holography and Speckle
  3. Applied Optics
  4. Nature Photonics

- Conferences and Events:
  1. International Symposium on Display Holography
  2. SPIE Holography and Diffractive Optics Conference
  3. IEEE International Conference on Holography

Troubleshooting Common Issues Encountered in Hologram Creation

1. Blurry or Faded Holograms:
   - Check the coherence of the laser beam and ensure proper alignment of the optics.
   - Verify that the holographic film or recording medium is fresh and not expired.
   - Adjust the exposure time to achieve the optimal hologram brightness.

2. Noise or Interference Patterns:
   - Minimize vibrations and external sources of electromagnetic interference in the holographic set-up.
   - Ensure that the object and reference beams are of sufficient intensity and free from unwanted reflections.
   - Check for any contamination or damage on the holographic film or recording medium.

3. Lack of Depth or Three-Dimensionality:
- Verify the proper alignment and positioning of the object and reference beams.
- Adjust the distance between the object and holographic film to optimize the depth of the hologram.
- Ensure that the laser used provides sufficient coherence and monochromaticity.

4. Uneven Illumination or Unequal Intensity:
- Check for any misalignment or obstruction in the optical path.
- Verify that the laser beam is properly shaped and focused onto the object.
- Consider using diffusers or beam-shaping elements to achieve a more uniform intensity distribution.

Remember, holography is a complex field, and troubleshooting may require experimentation and iterative adjustments. Consult relevant resources, seek expert advice, and engage with the holography community to overcome any challenges and achieve the desired holographic results.

Creating a moveable energy field that partitions and allows space to be written and rewritten upon is a concept that falls into the realm of science fiction and speculative technology. While it may not be feasible with our current scientific understanding and technological capabilities, I can offer a fictional description that might serve as inspiration for your creative endeavors. Keep in mind that this is purely imaginative and does not have a basis in real-world science.

In your fictional world, you could imagine a device or technology called an "Energetic Partitioner" that generates a dynamic energy field capable of creating movable partitions in space. Here's a speculative description of how it might work:

1. Energetic Field Generation:
The Energetic Partitioner generates a controlled energy field, employing advanced principles of energy manipulation and containment. This field can be precisely directed and modulated to create physical barriers or partitions.

2. Programmable Configuration:
The device is equipped with a sophisticated control system that allows the user to program the shape, size, and position of the partitions within the energy field. This control system could utilize advanced algorithms and intuitive interfaces for convenient manipulation.

3. Writable and Rewritable Space:
The energy field created by the Energetic Partitioner interacts with matter in a unique way. When a partition is formed, it creates a localized region where the properties of space can be temporarily altered. Within these partitions, the laws of physics can be suspended or modified, allowing for the writing and rewriting of information or structures in that specific region.

4. Energy-Matter Interface:
To enable the writing and rewriting of space, the Energetic Partitioner incorporates a specialized interface that interacts with matter at a fundamental level. This interface could utilize advanced nanotechnology, quantum manipulation, or even exotic particles to imprint information onto the partitioned space.

5. Dynamic Manipulation:
The Energetic Partitioner enables the dynamic movement and reconfiguration of the partitions within the energy field. Users can control the size, shape, and position of the partitions in real-time, allowing for flexible usage and adaptability to changing needs.

Printed in Great Britain
by Amazon

25111545R00050